The Politics of the Governed

THE LEONARD HASTINGS SCHOFF MEMORIAL LECTURES

The Politics of the Governed

Reflections on Popular Politics
in Most of the World

Partha Chatterjee

 COLUMBIA UNIVERSITY PRESS   NEW YORK

Columbia University Press

Publishers Since 1893

New York, Chichester, West Sussex

Copyright © 2004 Columbia University Press

All rights Reserved

Library of Congress Cataloging-in-Publication Data

Chatterjee, Partha, 1947–

The politics of the governed : reflections on popular politics in
   most of the world / Partha Chatterjee.

   p. cm. — (University seminars/Leonard Hastings Schoff
memorial lectures)

   Includes bibliographical references and index.

   ISBN 978-0-231-13062-2(cloth : alk. paper) –
   ISBN 978-0-231-13063-9 (pbk. : alk. paper)

   1. Politics, Practical—India. 2. Political participation—India.
3. Democracy—India. 4. Equality—India. 5. Citizenship—India.
I. Title. II. Series.

JQ281.C48 2004

320.954—dc22

                                                    2003060821

Columbia University Press books are printed on permanent and
durable acid-free paper

Printed in the United States of America

c 10 9 8 7 6 5 4 3 2
p 10 9 8 7 6 5 4 3

References to Internet Web Sites (URLs) were accurate at the
time of writing. Neither the author nor Columbia University
Press is responsible for Web sites that may have expired or
changed since the articles in this book were prepared.

*"The obstinate multitude yields last;
others vacillate endlessly."*

—*Apocryphal (early modern)*

*To Edward Said (1935–2003),
scholar extraordinary*

Contents

Photographs appear as an insert following page 78

Preface

The Leonard Hastings Schoff Memorial Lectures were delivered in November 2001. I am grateful to the University Seminars committee of Columbia University, and Robert Belknap in particular, for inviting me to deliver them. It was indeed an honor to follow the distinguished members of the Columbia faculty who had delivered these lectures before me. I am especially grateful to Akeel Bilgrami, Nicholas Dirks, Edward Said, and Gayatri Chakravorty Spivak for their warm and generous introductions to the lectures and to the members of the audience, including many of my students, for their enthusiastic participation in the discussions that followed. In preparing the lectures for publication, I have been mindful of many of the questions raised by my audience.

I must confess that it was a little daunting to speak under the giant shadow of what had happened in New York, in the United States, and in our hapless world in the weeks preceding the lectures. I could not claim to offer any spectacular enlightenment, and certainly not any magic solution to the world's intractable problems. What I did hope to bring to my audience then, and what I expect to present to my readers now, is a certain understanding—however hazy and indeterminate it may be—of what it is that is driving the energies and aspirations of numerous people in most of the world. This is not a world that is familiar to many of us, and I do not claim any privileged insider's knowledge. I have been, for the most part, myself an observer from the outside, except that for the greater part of the year when I live and work away from Columbia and New York, this world intrudes into my consciousness and declares its presence in ways that I cannot ignore. This is the world of popular politics in most of the world—the place where, I believe, political modernity is being forged today. It is both foolish and irresponsible to dismiss it contemptuously as the third world slum or the Arab street. There is politics here that is often contrary to the civil etiquette of metropolitan life, but it is insistent in its claims because, first, politics is numerous, and second, it is open to purposeful mobilization and leadership.

There is both a global and a local dimension to the politics of the governed. And there have been significant and interrelated changes along both dimensions in recent years. I have therefore decided to include in this volume four other lectures I have given in the last year that might help situate my understanding of political society in its larger global context as well as illustrate the possibilities and limits of political leadership in the present local context. These additional lectures may also provide an interesting change of perspective—from talking about politics in the Western academy to talking about it in "the East." It is a shift to which I am now so habituated that I am no longer conscious of the precise modalities of transference. I leave it to my readers to draw their own inferences.

I have been pursuing the idea of political society in most of the world for a few years now. Needless to say, I have benefited immensely from my discussions with many people at many places around the world. I began writing the present version of the lectures during a fellowship at the Wissenschaftskolleg in Berlin in 2001. I have also discussed with great profit earlier versions of these ideas in Bangalore, Calcutta, Cambridge (Massachusetts), Delhi, Hyderabad, Istanbul, Kathmandu, London, Paris, and Taipei. A small group consisting of Talal Asad, Carlos Forment, Mahmood Mamdani, and David Scott, with whom I would occasionally meet in New York to discuss each other's work was greatly stimulating. My colleagues on the editorial group of *Subaltern Studies* have been my intellectual companions for many years; I thank them all. As always, I am grateful to my colleagues at the Centre for Studies in Social Sciences, Calcutta, which is my place of work for the greater part of the year, for their friendship and support.

I thank Peter Dimock, Anne Routon, and Leslie Bialler of Columbia University Press for their help and understanding in supervising the publication of these lectures. I am also grateful to Ahmed Ali, Dilip Banerjee, Bikash Bose, Sabuj Mukhopadhyay and Fr. P. J. Joseph of Chitrabani for granting me permission to use their photographs in this book. Abhijit Bhattacharya of the archives and the staff of the library of the Centre for Studies in Social Sciences, Calcutta, have been, as always, immensely helpful: I thank them all.

Calcutta
March 31, 2003

The Politics of the Governed

PART I

THE LEONARD HASTINGS SCHOFF
MEMORIAL LECTURES
2001

ONE

The Nation in Heterogeneous Time

I

My subject is popular politics in most of the world. When I say "popular," I do not necessarily presume any particular institutional form or process of politics. I do, however, suggest that much of the politics I describe is conditioned by the functions and activities of modern governmental systems that have now become part of the expected functions of governments everywhere. These expectations and activities have produced, I will argue, certain relations between governments and populations. The popular politics I will describe grows upon and is shaped by those relations. What I mean by "most of world" will, I hope, become clearer as I proceed. I mean, in a general sense, those parts of the world that were not direct participants in the history of the evolution of the institutions of modern capitalist democracy. "Modern capitalist democracy" might, in a loose way, be taken to mean the modern West. But, as I will indicate, the modern West has a significant presence in many modern non-Western societies, just as, indeed, there are large sectors of contemporary Western society that are not necessarily part of the historical entity known as the modern West. However, if I were to make a rough estimate of the number of people in the world who would be, in a conceptual sense, included within my description of popular politics, I would say that I am talking of the political life of well over three-fourths of contemporary humanity.

The familiar concepts of social theory that I will need to revisit here are civil society and state, citizenship and rights, universal affiliations and particular identities. Since I will look at popular politics, I must also consider the question of democracy. Many of these concepts will no longer look familiar after I position my lenses and persuade you to look through them. Civil society, for instance, will appear as the closed association of modern elite groups, sequestered from the wider popular life of the communities, walled up within enclaves of civic freedom and rational law. Citizenship will take on two different shapes—the formal and the real. And unlike the old way, known to us from the Greeks to Machiavelli to Marx, of talking about the rulers and the ruled, I will invite you to think of those who govern and those who are governed. Governance, that new buzzword in policy studies, is, I will suggest, the body of knowledge and set of techniques used by, or on behalf of, those who govern. Democracy today, I will insist, is not government of, by and for the people. Rather, it should be seen as the politics of the governed.

I will clarify and elaborate on my conceptual arguments in chapter 2. To introduce my discussion of popular politics, let me begin by posing for you a conflict that lies at the heart of modern politics in most of the world. It is the opposition between the universal ideal of civic nationalism, based on individual freedoms and equal rights irrespective of distinctions of religion, race, language, or culture, and the particular demands of cultural identity, which call for the differential treatment of particular groups on grounds of vulnerability or backwardness or historical injustice, or indeed for numerous other reasons. The opposition, I will argue, is symptomatic of the transition that occurred in modern politics in the course of the twentieth century from a conception of democratic politics grounded in the idea of popular sovereignty to one in which democratic politics is shaped by governmentality.

Benedict Anderson captured the universal ideal of civic nationalism well when he argued, in his now classic *Imagined Communities*, that the nation lives in homogeneous empty time.[1] In this, he was, in fact, following a dominant strand in modern historical thinking that imagines the social space of modernity as distributed in homogeneous empty time. A Marxist could call this the time of capital. Anderson explicitly adopts the formulation from Walter Benjamin and uses it to brilliant effect to show the material possibilities of large anonymous socialities being formed by the simultaneous experience of reading the daily newspaper or following the private lives of popular fictional characters. It is the same simultaneity experienced in homogeneous empty time that allows us to speak of the reality of such categories of political economy as prices, wages, markets, and so on. Empty homogeneous time is the time of capital. Within its domain, capital allows for no resistance to its free movement. When it encounters an impediment, it thinks it has encountered another time—something out of pre-capital, something that belongs to the pre-modern. Such resistances to capital (or to modernity) are therefore understood as coming out of humanity's past, something people should have left behind but somehow haven't. But by imagining capital (or modernity) as an attribute of time itself, this view succeeds not only in branding the resistances to it as archaic and backward, but also in securing for capital and modernity their ultimate triumph, regardless of what some people may believe or hope, because after all, time does not stand still.

In his recent book *The Spectre of Comparisons*, Anderson has followed up his analysis in *Imagined Communities* by distinguishing between nationalism and the politics of ethnicity. He does this by identifying two kinds of seriality that are produced by the modern imaginings of community. One is the unbound seriality of the everyday universals of modern social thought: nations, citizens, revolutionaries, bureaucrats, workers, intellectuals, and so on. The other is the bound seriality of governmentality: the finite totals of enumerable classes of population produced by the modern census and the modern electoral systems. Unbound serialities are typically imagined and narrated by means of the classic instruments of print-capitalism, namely, the newspaper and the novel. They afford the opportunity for individuals to imagine themselves as members of larger than face-to-face solidarities, of choosing to act on behalf of those solidarities, of transcending by an act of political imagination the limits imposed by traditional practices. Unbound serialities are potentially liberating. Bound serialities, by contrast, can operate only with integers. This implies that for each category of classification, any individual can count only as one or zero, never as a fraction, which in turn means that all partial or mixed affiliations to a category are ruled out. One can only be black or not black, Muslim or not Muslim, tribal or not tribal, never only partially or contextually so. Bound serialities, Anderson suggests, are constricting and perhaps inherently conflictual. They produce the tools of ethnic politics.

Anderson uses this distinction between bound and unbound serialities to make his argument about the residual goodness of nationalism and the unrelieved nastiness of ethnic politics. Clearly, he is keen to preserve what is genuinely ethical and noble in the universalist critical thought characteristic of the Enlightenment. Faced with the indubitable facts of historical conflict and change, the aspiration here is to affirm an ethical universal that does not deny the variability of human wants and values, or cast them aside as unworthy or ephemeral, but rather encompasses and integrates them as the real historical ground on which that ethical universal must be established. Anderson, in the tradition of much progressive historicist thinking in the twentieth century, sees the politics of universalism as something that belongs to the very character of the time in which we live. He speaks of "the remarkable planetary spread, not merely of nationalism, but of a profoundly standardized conception of politics, in part by reflecting on the everyday practices, rooted in industrial material civilization, that have displaced the cosmos to make way for the world."[2] Such a conception of politics requires an understanding of the world as *one*, so that a common activity called politics can be seen to be going on *everywhere*. One should note that time in this conception easily translates into space, so that we should indeed speak here of the time-space of modernity. Thus, politics, in this sense, inhabits the empty homogeneous time-space of modernity.

I disagree. I believe this view of modernity, or indeed of capital, is mistaken because it is one-sided. It looks at only one dimension of the time-space of modern life. People can only imagine themselves in empty homogeneous time; they do not live in it. Empty homogeneous time is the utopian time of capital. It linearly connects past, present, and future, creating the possibility for all of those historicist imaginings of identity, nationhood, progress, and so on that Anderson, along with many others, have made familiar to us. But empty homogeneous time is not located anywhere in real space—it is utopian. The real space of modern life consists of heterotopia. (My debt to Michel Foucault should be obvious, even if I am not always faithful to his use of this term.)[3] Time here is heterogeneous, unevenly dense. Here, even industrial workers do not all internalize the work-discipline of capitalism, and more curiously, even when they do, they do not do so in the same way. Politics here does not mean the same thing to all people. To ignore this is, I believe, to discard the real for the utopian.

Homi Bhabha, describing the location of the nation in temporality, pointed out a few years ago how the narrative of the nation tended to be split into a double time and hence an inevitable ambivalence: in one, the people were an object of national pedagogy because they were always in the making, in a process of historical progress, not yet fully developed to fulfill the nation's destiny; but in the other, the unity of the people, their permanent identification with the nation, had to be continually signified, repeated, and performed.[4] I will illustrate some of the instances of this ambivalence and argue that they are an inevitable aspect of modern politics itself. To disavow them is either wishful piety or an endorsement of the existing structure of dominance within the nation.

It is possible to cite many examples from the postcolonial world that suggest the presence of a dense and heterogeneous time. In those places, one could show industrial capitalists delaying the closing of a business deal because they hadn't yet heard from their respective astrologers, or industrial workers who would not touch a new machine until it had been consecrated with appropriate religious rites, or voters who would set fire to themselves to mourn the defeat of their favorite leader, or ministers who openly boast of having secured more jobs for people from their own clan and having kept the others out. To call this the co-presence of several times—the time of the modern and the times of the pre-modern—is only to endorse the utopianism of Western modernity. Much recent ethnographic work has established that these "other" times are not mere survivors from a premodern past: they are new products of the encounter with modernity itself. One must, therefore, call it the heterogeneous time of modernity. And to push my polemical point a little further, I will add that the postcolonial world outside Western Europe and North America actually constitutes *most* of the populated modern world.

Let me discuss in some detail an example of the continuing tension between the utopian dimension of the homogeneous time of capital and the real space constituted by the heterogeneous time of governmentality and the effects produced by this tension on efforts to narrativize the nation.

II

Bhimrao Ramji Ambedkar (1891–1956) was one of Columbia University's more remarkable students. Born into the untouchable Mahar community of Maharashtra in India, he fought against stupendous odds to seek higher education and qualify for a professional career. He got a Ph.D. in Political Science from Columbia University in 1917 and always remembered the influence on him of his professors John Dewey and Edwin Seligman.[5] He is famous in India as the foremost political leader in the twentieth century of the downtrodden Dalit peoples—the former untouchable castes. In this role, he has been both celebrated and vilified for having strenuously fought for the separate political representation of the Dalits, for preferential reservation or affirmative action in their favor in education and government employment, and for constructing their distinct cultural identity going as far as conversion to another religion—Buddhism. At the same time, Ambedkar is also famous as the principal architect of the Indian constitution, a staunch advocate of the interventionist modernizing state and of the legal protection of the modern virtues of equal citizenship and secularism. Seldom has been the tension between utopian homogeneity and real heterogeneity played out more dramatically than in the intellectual and political career of B. R. Ambedkar.

My focus here will be on certain moments in Ambedkar's life, in order to highlight the contradictions posed for a modern politics by the rival demands of universal citizenship on the one hand and the protection of particularist rights on the other. My burden will be to show that there is no available historical narrative of the nation that can resolve those contradictions.

Ambedkar was an unalloyed modernist. He believed in science, history, rationality, secularism, and above all in the modern state as the site for the actualization of human reason. But as an intellectual of the Dalit peoples, he could not but confront the question: what is the reason for the unique form of social inequality practiced within the so-called caste system of India? In two major works, *Who Were the Shudras* (1946) and *The Untouchables* (1948), Ambedkar looked for the specific historical origin of untouchability.[6] He concluded that untouchability did not go back to times immemorial; it had a definite history that could be scientifically established to be no longer than about 1500 years.

It is not necessary for us here to judge the plausibility of Ambedkar's theory. What is more interesting for our purposes is the narrative structure it suggests. He argued that there was, in the beginning, a state of equality between the Brahmins, the Shudras, and the untouchables. This equality, moreover, was not in some mythological state of nature but at a definite historical moment when all Indo-Aryan tribes were nomadic pastoralists. Then came the stage of settled agriculture and the reaction, in the form of Buddhism, to the sacrificial religion of the Vedic tribes. This was followed by the conflict between the Brahmins and the Buddhists, leading to the political defeat of Buddhism, the degradation of the Shudras, and the relegation of the beef-eating "broken men" into untouchability. The modern struggle for the abolition of caste was thus a quest for a return to that primary equality that was the original historical condition of the nation. The utopian search for homogeneity is thus made historical. It is, as we know, a familiar historicist narrative of modern nationalism.

To show how this narrative is disrupted by the heterogeneous time of colonial governmentality, let me turn to the fiction of nationalism.

III

One of the greatest modernist novels about Indian nationalism is *Dhorai charitmanas* (1949–51) by the Bengali writer Satinath Bhaduri (1906–1965).[7] The novel is deliberately constructed to fit the form of the *Ramcharitmanas*, the retelling in Hindi by the sixteenth-century saint-poet Tulsidas (1532–1623) of the epic story of Rama, the mythical king who, through his exemplary life and conduct, is supposed to have created the most perfect kingdom on earth. Tulsidas's Ramayana is perhaps the most widely known literary work in the vast Hindi-speaking regions of India, providing an everyday language of moral discourse that cut across caste, class, and sectarian divides. It is also said to have been the most powerful vehicle for the generalization of Brahminical cultural values in northern India. The distinctness of Satinath Bhaduri's modernist retelling of the epic is that its hero, Dhorai, is from one of the backward castes.

Dhorai is a Tatma from northern Bihar (the district is Purnea, but Satinath gives it the fictional name Jirania). It is not an agriculturist group, specializing instead in the thatching of roofs and the digging of wells. When Dhorai was a child, his father died, and when his mother wanted to remarry, she left him in the charge of Bauka Bawa, the village holy man. Dhorai grew up going from door to door, accompanying the sadhu with his begging bowl, singing songs, mostly about the legendary king Rama and his perfect kingdom. The mental world of Dhorai is steeped in mythic time. He never goes to school but knows that those who can read the Ramayana are men of great merit and social authority. His elders—those around him—know of the government, of course, and know of the courts and the police, and some in the neighborhood who worked in the gardens and kitchens of the officials could even tell you when the district magistrate was displeased with the chairman of the district board or when the new kitchen maid was spending a little too much time in the evenings in the police officer's bungalow. But their general strategy of survival, perfected over generations of experience, is to stay away from entanglements with government and its procedures. Once, following a feud, the residents of the neighboring hamlet of Dhangars set fire to Bauka Bawa's hut. The police come to investigate and Dhorai, the sole eyewitness, is asked to describe what he had seen. As he is about to speak, he notices Bauka Bawa's eyes. "Don't talk," the Bawa seems to say. "This is the police, they'll go away in an hour. The Dhangars are our neighbors, we'll have to live with them." Dhorai understands and tells the police that he had seen nothing and did not know who had set fire to their house.

One day, Dhorai, along with others in the village, hear of Ganhi Bawa who, it was said, was a bigger holy man than their own Bauka Bawa or indeed any Bawa they had known, because he was almost as big as Lord Rama himself. Ganhi Bawa, they heard, ate neither meat nor fish, had never married and roamed around completely naked. Even the Bengali schoolmaster, the most learned man in the area, had become Ganhi Bawa's follower. Soon there is a sensation in the village when it is found that an image of Ganhi Bawa had appeared on a pumpkin. With great festivity, the miraculous pumpkin is installed in the village temple and offerings are made to the greatest holy man in the country. Ganhi Bawa, the Tatmas agreed, was a great soul indeed because even the Muslims promised to stop eating meat and onions, and the village shaman, whom no one had ever seen sober, vowed henceforth to drink only the lightest toddy and to stay away completely from opium. Some time later, a few villagers went all the way to the district town to see Ganhi Bawa himself, and came back with their enthusiasm somewhat deflated. The huge crowds had prevented them from seeing the great man from close but what they had seen was incongruous. Ganhi Bawa, they reported, like the fancy lawyers and teachers in town, wore spectacles! Who had ever seen a holy man wear spectacles? One or two even whispered if the man might not, after all, be a fake.

Satinath Bhaduri's intricately crafted account of Dhorai's upbringing among the Tatmas in the early decades of the twentieth century could be easily read as a faithful ethnography of colonial governance and the nationalist movement in northern India. We know, for instance, from Shahid Amin's studies how the authority of Mahatma Gandhi was constructed among India's peasantry through stories of his miraculous powers and rumors about the fate of his followers and detractors, or how the Congress program and the objectives of the movement were themselves transmitted in the countryside in the language of myth and popular religion.[8] If Gandhi and the movements he led in the 1920s and 1930s were a set of common events that connected the lives of millions of people in both the cities and the villages of India, they did not constitute a common experience. Rather, even as they participated in what historians describe as the same great events, their own understandings of those events were narrated in very different languages and inhabited very different lifeworlds. The nation, even if it was being constituted through such events, existed only in heterogeneous time.

Of course, it might be objected that the nation is indeed an abstraction, that it is, to use the phrase that Ben Anderson has made famous, only "an imagined community" and that, therefore, this ideal and empty construct, floating as it were in homogeneous time, can be given a varied content by diverse groups of people, all of whom, remaining different in their concrete locations, can nevertheless become elements in the unbound seriality of national citizens. Without doubt, this is the dream of all nationalists. Satinath Bhaduri, who was himself a leading functionary in the Congress organization in Purnea district, shared the dream. He was acutely aware of the narrowness and particularism of the everyday lives of his characters. They were yet to become national citizens, but he was hopeful of change. He saw that even the lowly Tatmas and Dhangars were stirring. His hero Dhorai leads the Tatmas into defying the local Brahmins and wearing the sacred thread themselves—in a process, occurring all over India at this time, that the sociologist M. N. Srinivas describes as Sanskritization, but which the historian David Hardiman has shown to be marked by a bitterly contested and often violent struggle over elite domination and subaltern resistance.[9] The intricate caste and communal grid of governmental classifications is never absent from Satinath's narrative. But in a deliberate allusion to the life-story of the legendary Prince Rama, Satinath throws his hero Dhorai into a cruel conspiracy hatched against him by his kinsmen. He suspects his wife of having a liaison with a Christian man from the Dhangar hamlet. He leaves the village, goes into exile and resumes his life in another village, among other communities. Dhorai is uprooted from the narrowness of his home and thrown into the world. The new metalled roadway, along which motorcars and trucks now whizz past ponderous bullock-carts, opens up his imagination. "Where does this road begin? Where does it end? [Dhorai] doesn't know. Perhaps no one knows. Some of the carts are loaded with maize, others bring plaintiffs to the district court, still others carry patients to the hospital. In his mind, Dhorai sees shadows that suggest to him something of the vastness of the country."[10] The nation is coming into shape. Satinath sends off his hero into an epic journey toward the promised goal, not of kingdom because this is no longer the mythical age of Rama, but of citizenship.

IV

Ambedkar's dream of equal citizenship also had to contend with the fact of governmental classifications. As early as 1920, he had posed the problem of representation faced by untouchables in India: "The right of representation and the right to hold office under the state are the two most important rights that make up citizenship. But the untouchability of the untouchables puts these rights far beyond their reach. . . . they [the untouchables] can be represented by the untouchables alone." The general representation of all citizens would not serve the special requirements of the untouchables, because given the prejudices and entrenched practices among the dominant castes, there was no reason to expect that the latter would use the law to emancipate the untouchables. "A legislature composed of high caste men will not pass a law removing untouchability, sanctioning intermarriages, removing the ban on the use of public streets, public temples, public schools. . . . This is not because they cannot, but chiefly because they will not."[11]

But there were several ways in which the special needs of representation of the untouchables could be secured, and many of these had been tried out in colonial India. One was the protection by colonial officials of the interests of the lower castes against the politically dominant upper castes or the nomination by the colonial government of distinguished men from the untouchable groups to serve as their representatives. Another way was to reserve a certain number of seats in the legislature only for candidates from the lower castes. Yet another was to have separate electorates of lower-caste voters who could elect their own representatives. In the immensely complicated world of late colonial constitutional politics in India, all of these methods, with innumerable variations, were debated and tried out. Besides, caste was not the only contentious issue of ethnic representation; the even more divisive issue of religious minorities became inextricably tied up with the politics of citizenship in late colonial India.

Ambedkar clearly ruled out one of these methods of special representation—protection by the colonial regime. In 1930, when the Congress declared independence or Swaraj as its political goal, Ambedkar declared at a conference of the depressed classes:

> the bureaucratic form of Government in India should be replaced by a Government which will be a Government of the people, by the people and for the people. . . . We feel that nobody can remove our grievances as well as we can, and we cannot remove them unless we get political power in our own hands. No share of this political power can evidently come to us so long as the British government remains as it is. It is only in a Swaraj constitution that we stand any chance of getting the political power in our own hands, without which we cannot bring salvation to our people. . . . We know that political power is passing from the British into the hands of those who wield such tremendous economic, social and religious sway over our existence. We are willing that it may happen, though the idea of Swaraj recalls to the mind of many the tyrannies, oppressions and injustices practiced upon us in the past.[12]

The dilemma is clearly posed here. The colonial government, for all its homilies about the need to uplift those oppressed by the religious tyranny of traditional Hinduism, could only look after the untouchables as its subjects. It could never give them citizenship. Only under an independent national constitution was citizenship conceivable for the untouchables. Yet, if independence meant the rule of the upper castes, how could the untouchables expect equal citizenship and the end of the social tyranny from which they had suffered for centuries? Ambedkar's position was clear: the untouchables must support national independence, in the full knowledge that it would lead to the political dominance of the upper castes, but they must press on with the struggle for equality within the framework of the new constitution.

In 1932, the method of achieving equal citizenship for the untouchables became the issue in a dramatic standoff between Ambedkar and Gandhi. In the course of negotiations between the British government and Indian political leaders on constitutional reforms, Ambedkar, representing the so-called depressed classes, had argued that they must be allowed to constitute a separate electorate and elect their own representatives to the central and provincial legislatures. The Congress, which had by this time conceded a similar demand for separate electorates for the Muslims, refused to accept that the untouchables were a community separate from the Hindus and was prepared instead to have reserved seats for them to be chosen by the general electorate. Ambedkar clarified that he would be prepared to accept this formula if there was any hope that the British would grant universal adult suffrage to all Indians. But since the suffrage was severely limited by property and education qualifications, the depressed castes, dispersed as a thin minority within the general population and, unlike the Muslim minority, lacking any significant territorial concentrations, were unlikely to have any influence at all over the elections. The only way to ensure that the legislature contained at least some who were the true representatives of the untouchables was to allow them to be elected by a separate electorate of the depressed classes.

Gandhi reacted fiercely to Ambedkar's suggestion that upper-caste Congress leaders could never properly represent the untouchables, calling it "the unkindest cut of all." Indulging in a rather un-mahatma-like boast, he declared: "I claim myself in my own person to represent the vast mass of the Untouchables. Here I speak not merely on behalf of the Congress, but I speak on my own behalf, and I claim that I would get, if there was a referendum of the Untouchables, their vote, and that I would top the poll." He insisted that unlike the question of the religious minorities, the issue of untouchability was a matter internal to Hinduism and had to be resolved within it.

I do not mind Untouchables, if they so desire, being converted to Islam or Christianity. I should tolerate that, but I cannot possibly tolerate what is in store for Hinduism if there are two divisions set forth in the villages. Those who speak of the political rights of Untouchables do not know their India, do not know how Indian society is today constructed, and therefore I want to say with all the emphasis that I can command that if I was the only person to resist this thing I would resist it with my life.

True to his word, Gandhi threatened to go on a fast rather than concede the demand for separate electorates for the depressed classes. Put under enormous pressure, Ambedkar conceded and, after negotiations, signed with Gandhi what is known as the Poona Pact by which the Dalits were given a substantial number of reserved seats but within the Hindu electorate.[13] As it happened, this remained the basic form for the representation of the former untouchable castes in the constitution of independent India, but of course, by this time the country had been divided into two sovereign nation-states.

The problem of national homogeneity and minority citizenship was posed and temporarily resolved in India in the early 1930s. But the form of the resolution is instructive. It graphically illustrates that ambivalence of the nation as a narrative strategy as well as an apparatus of power which, as Homi Bhabha has pointed out, "produces a continual slippage into analogous, even metonymic, categories, like the people, minorities, or 'cultural difference' that continually overlap in the act of writing the nation."[14] Ambedkar, as we have seen, had no quarrel with the idea of the homogeneous nation as a pedagogical category—the nation as progress, the nation in the process of becoming—except that he would have insisted with Gandhi and the other Congress leaders that it was not just the ignorant masses that needed training in proper citizenship but the upper-caste elite as well which had still not accepted that democratic equality was incompatible with caste inequality. But Ambedkar refused to join Gandhi in performing that homogeneity in constitutional negotiations over citizenship. The untouchables, he insisted, were a minority within the nation and needed special representation in the political body. On the other hand, Gandhi and the Congress, while asserting that the nation was one and indivisible, had already conceded that the Muslims were a minority within the nation. The untouchables? They represented a problem internal to Hinduism. Imperceptibly, the homogeneity of India slides into the homogeneity of the Hindus. The removal of untouchability remains a pedagogical task, to be accomplished by social reform, if necessary by law, but caste inequality among the Hindus is not to be performed before the British rulers or the Muslim minority. Homogeneity breaks down on one plane, only to be reasserted on another. Heterogeneity, unstoppable at one point, is forcibly suppressed at another.

In the meantime, our fictional hero Dhorai continues, in the 1930s, to receive his education in nationalism. Loosened from his moorings, he drifts to another village and starts life afresh among the Koeri, a backward caste of sharecroppers and laborers. Dhorai begins to learn the realities of peasant life—of Rajput landlords and Koeri adhiars and Santal laborers, of growing paddy and jute and tobacco and maize, of moneylenders and traders. In January 1934, Bihar is ripped apart by the most violent earthquake in its recorded history. Government officers come to survey the damage; so do the nationalist volunteers from the Congress. For more than a year, the Koeris hear vaguely that they were going to be given "relief." And then they are told that the survey had found that the Koeri huts, being made of mud walls and thatched roofs, had been easily repaired by the Koeris themselves, but the brick houses of the Rajput landlords had suffered severe damage. The report had recommended, therefore, that the bulk of the relief should be given to the Rajputs.

Thus begins a new chapter in Dhorai's education—his discovery that the Bengali lawyers and Rajput landlords were fast becoming the principal followers of the Mahatma. But even as the old exploiters become the new messengers of national freedom, the mystique of the Mahatma remains untarnished. One day, a volunteer arrives in the village with letters from the Mahatma. He tells the Koeris that they in turn must send a letter each to the Mahatma. No, no, they don't have to pay for the postage stamp. All they have to do is walk up to the officer who would give them a letter which they must put in Mahatmaji's postbox—the white one, remember, not the colored ones. This was called the "vote." The volunteer instructs Dhorai:

"Your name is Dhorai Koeri, your father is Kirtu Koeri. Remember to say that to the officer. Your father is Kirtu Koeri." Dhorai does as he is told.

Inside the voting booth, Dhorai stood with folded hands in front of the white box and dropped the letter into it. Praise to Mahatmaji, praise to the Congress volunteer, they had given Dhorai the little role of the squirrel in the great task of building the kingdom of Rama. But his heart broke with sorrow—if only he could write, he would have written the letter himself to the Mahatma. Just imagine, all these people writing letters to the Mahatma, from one end of the country to the other, all together, at the same time. Tatmatuli, Jirania, ... Dhorai, ... the volunteer, ... they all wanted the same thing. They had all sent the same letter to the Mahatma. The government, the officers, the police, the landlords, ... all were against them. They belonged to many different castes, and yet they had come so close. . . . They were linked as though by a spider's web; the fibre was so thin that if you tried to grab it, it would break. Indeed, you couldn't always tell if it was there or not. When it swayed gently in the breeze, or the morning dewdrops clung to it, or when a sudden ray of the sun fell on it, you saw it, and even then only for a moment. This was the land of Ramji over which his avatar Mahatmaji was weaving his thin web. . . . "Hey, what are you doing inside the booth?" The officer's voice broke his reverie. Dhorai came out quickly.[15]

The vote is the great anonymous performance of citizenship, which is why it probably did not matter too much that Dhorai's introduction to this ritual was through an act of impersonation. But it only concealed the question of who represents whom within the nation. Although the Koeris voted faithfully for the Mahatma, they were dismayed to find that the Rajput landlord with whom they had fought for years was elected chairman of the district board with support from the Congress. Mahatmaji's men, they heard, were now ministers in the government, but when a new road was built, sure enough, it went right next to the Rajput houses.

But Dhorai bought himself a copy of the Ramayana. One day, he promised himself, he would learn to read it. The passage to the kingdom of Rama, however, was suddenly disrupted when news arrived that the Mahatma had been arrested by the British. This was the final struggle, the Mahatma had announced. Every true follower of Mahatmaji must now join his army. Yes, the army; they must act against the tyrants, not wait to be arrested. Dhorai is mobilized into the Quit India movement of 1942. This was a war unlike any other; it was, the volunteers said, a revolution. Together, they stormed the police station, setting fire to it. By the morning, the district magistrate, the police superintendent, and all senior officers had fled. Victory to Mahatmaji, victory to the revolution! The district had won independence; they were free.

It didn't last long. Weeks later, the troops moved in, with trucks and guns. Along with the volunteers, Dhorai left for the forests. He was now a wanted man, a rebel. But they were all wanted men—they were Mahatmaji's soldiers. There was a strange equality among them in the forest. They had dropped their original names and called each other Gandhi, Jawahar, Patel, Azad—they were so many anonymous replicas of the representatives of the nation. Except they had been driven away from its everyday life. Sometime later, word came that the British had won the war with the Germans and the Japanese, the Congress leaders were about to be released and all revolutionaries must surrender. Surrender? And be tried and jailed? Who knows, may be even hanged? Dhorai's unit resolves not to surrender.

v

On the national stage, the Muslim League resolved in March 1940 that any constitutional plan for devolution of power in India must include an arrangement by which geographically contiguous areas with Muslim majorities could be grouped into independent states, autonomous and sovereign. This became known as the Pakistan resolution. The Congress opposed the plan. A few months later, in December 1940, Ambedkar wrote a long book entitled *Pakistan or Partition of India* in which he discussed in detail the pros and cons of the proposal.[16]

It is a book that is, surprisingly, seldom mentioned, even today when there is such a great Ambedkar revival.[17] In addition to showing his superb skills as a political analyst and a truly astonishing prescience, I think it is a text in which Ambedkar grappled most productively with the twofold demand on his politics—one, to further the struggle for universal and equal citizenship within the nation, and two, to secure special representation for the depressed castes in the body politic.

The book is almost Socratic in its dialogical structure, presenting first, in the strongest possible terms, the Muslim case for Pakistan, and then the Hindu case against Pakistan, and then considering the alternatives available to the Muslims and the Hindus if there were no partition. What is striking is the way in which Ambedkar, as the unstated representative of the untouchables, adopts a position of perfect neutrality in the debate, with no stake at all in how the matter is resolved—he belongs neither to the Muslim nor to the Hindu side. All he is concerned with is to judge the rival arguments and recommend what seems to him the most realistic solution. But, of course, this is only a narrative strategy. We know that Ambedkar did have a great stake in the question: the most important issue for him was whether or not partition would be better for the untouchables of India. The significance of *Pakistan or Partition of India* is that Ambedkar is here judging the utopian claims of nationhood in the concrete terms of realist politics.

After dissecting the arguments of both sides, Ambedkar comes to the conclusion that, on balance, partition would be better for both Muslims and Hindus. The clinching arguments come when he considers the alternative to partition: how was a united and independent India, free from British rule, likely to be governed? Given the hostility of Muslims to the idea of a single central government, inevitably dominated by the Hindu majority, it was certain that if there were no partition, India would have to live with a weak central government, with most powers devolved to the provinces. It would be "an anaemic and sickly state." The animosities and mutual suspicions would remain: "burying Pakistan is not the same thing as burying the ghost of Pakistan."[18] Moreover, there was the question of the armed forces

of independent India. In a long chapter, Ambedkar goes straight to
the heart of colonial governance and discusses the communal composition of the British Indian army, a subject on which there was a
virtual conspiracy of silence. He points out that almost sixty percent
of the Indian army consisted of men from the Punjab, the North-
West Frontier and Kashmir, and of them more than half were Muslims. Would a weak central government, regarded with suspicion by
the Muslim population, command the loyalty of these troops? On the
other hand, should the new government attempt to change the communal composition of the army, would that be accepted without protest by the Muslims of the north-west?[19]

Judged positively, the new state of Pakistan would be a homogeneous state. The boundaries of Punjab and Bengal could be redrawn
to form relatively homogeneous Muslim and Hindu regions to be
integrated with Pakistan and India, respectively. Long before anyone
had demanded the partition of the two provinces, Ambedkar foresaw
that the Hindus and Sikhs would not agree to live in a country specifically created for Muslims and would want to join India. For the
North-West Frontier Province and Sind, where the Hindu population
was thinly distributed, the only realistic solution was an officially supervised transfer of population, as had happened in Turkey, Greece,
and Bulgaria. The India or Hindustan that would be created would
be composite, not homogeneous. But the minority question could
then be handled more reasonably. "To me, it seems that if Pakistan
does not solve the communal problem within Hindustan, it substan-
tially reduces its proportion and makes it of minor significance and
much easier of peaceful solution."[20]

And then, in a string of brilliant moves of real-political logic,
Ambedkar shows that only in united India, in which more than a
third of the population is Muslim, could Hindu dominance be a serious threat. In such a state, the Muslims, fearing the tyranny of the
majority, would organize themselves into a Muslim party such as the
Muslim League, provoking in turn the rise of Hindu parties calling
for Hindu Raj. Following partition, on the other hand, the Muslims
in Hindustan would be a small and widely scattered minority. They
would inevitably join this or that political party, pursuing different

social and economic programs. Similarly, there would be little ground
left for a party like the Hindu Mahasabha, which would wither away.
And as for the lower orders of Hindu society, they would make common cause with the Muslim minority to fight the Hindu high castes
for their rights of citizenship and social dignity.[21]
We need not spend time trying to assess the intrinsic merits of
Ambedkar's arguments for and against the partition of India, although in the discursive context of the early 1940s they are remarkably
perspicacious. I am emphasizing here the ground on which he lays
his arguments. He is fully aware of the value of universal and equal
citizenship and wholly endorses the ethical significance of unbound
serialities. On the other hand, he realizes that the slogan of univer-
sality is often a mask to cover the perpetuation of real inequalities.
The politics of democratic nationhood offers a means for achieving a
more substantive equality, but only by ensuring adequate representation for the underprivileged groups within the body politic. A strategic
politics of groups, classes, communities, ethnicities—bound serialities
of all sorts—is thus inevitable. Homogeneity is not thereby forsaken;
on the contrary, in specific contexts, it can often supply the clue to a
strategic solution, such as partition, to a problem of intractable heterogeneity. On the other hand, unlike the utopian claims of universalist
nationalism, the politics of heterogeneity can never claim to yield a
general formula for all peoples at all times: its solutions are always
strategic, contextual, historically specific and, inevitably, provisional.

Let me then finally return to Anderson's distinction between nationalism and the politics of ethnicity. He agrees that the "bound
serialities" of governmentality can create a sense of community, which
is precisely what the politics of ethnic identity feeds on. But this sense
of community, Anderson thinks, is illusory. In these real and imagined
censuses, "thanks to capitalism, state machineries and mathematics,
integral bodies become identical, and thus serially aggregable as phan-
tom communities."[22] By contrast, the "unbound serialities" of nationalism do not, one presumes, need to turn the free individual
members of the national community into integers. It can imagine the
nation as having existed in identical form from the dawn of historical
time to the present without requiring a census-like verification of its

identity. It can also experience the simultaneity of the imagined collective life of the nation without imposing rigid and arbitrary criteria of membership. Can such "unbound serialities" exist anywhere except in utopian space?

To endorse these "unbound serialities" while rejecting the "bound" ones is, in fact, to imagine nationalism without modern governmentality. What modern politics can we have that has no truck with capitalism, state machineries, or mathematics? The historical moment that Anderson, and many others, seem keen to preserve is the mythical moment when classical nationalism merges with modernity. I believe it is no longer productive to reassert the utopian politics of classical nationalism. Or rather, I do not believe it is an option that is available for a theorist from the postcolonial world. Such a theorist must chart a course that steers away from global cosmopolitanism on the one hand and ethnic chauvinism on the other. It means necessarily to dirty one's hands in the complicated business of the politics of governmentality. The asymmetries produced and legitimized by the universalisms of modern nationalism have not left room for any ethically neat choice here. For the postcolonial theorist, like the postcolonial novelist, is born only when the mythical timespace of epic modernity has been lost forever.

Let me end by describing the fate of our fictional hero Dhorai. Living in the forests with his band of fugitive rebels, Dhorai is brought face to face with the limits to his dreams of equality and freedom. It is not the bound serialities of caste and community that prove illusory, but rather the promise of equal citizenship. The harshness of fugitive life scrapes the veneer off the shell of comradeship and the old hierarchies reappear. Suspicion, intrigue, revenge and recrimination become the ruling sentiments. Dhorai's copy of the Ramayana lies tied up in his bundle, unopened, unread. In the middle of all this, a young boy joins the band. He is a Christian Dhangar, he says, from the hamlet next to Tatmatuli. Dhorai feels a strange bond with the boy. Might he be, he imagines, the son he has never seen? Dhorai looks after the boy and asks him many questions. The more he talks to him, the more he is convinced that this indeed is his son. The boy falls ill, and Dhorai decides to take him to his mother. As he approaches

Tatmatuli, he can hardly control his excitement. Was this going to be the epic dénouement of the latter-day untouchable Rama? Was he going to be united with his banished wife and son? The mother appears, takes her son in, comes out again and invites the kind stranger to sit down. She talks about her son, about her dead husband. Dhorai listens to her. She is someone else, not his wife. The boy is someone else, not his son. Dhorai makes polite conversation for a few minutes and then goes, we don't know where. But he leaves behind his bundle, along with the copy of the Ramayana for which he has no further need. Dhorai has lost forever his promised place in prophetic time.

Or has he? Following independence, B. R. Ambedkar became chairman of the drafting committee of the Indian constitution and later the minister of law. In these capacities, he was instrumental in putting together one of the most progressive democratic constitutions in the world, guaranteeing the fundamental rights of freedom and equality irrespective of religion or caste and at the same providing for special representation in the legislatures for the formerly untouchable castes.[23] But changing the law was one thing; changing social practices was another matter. Frustrated by the ineffectiveness of the state in putting an end to caste discrimination in Hindu society, Ambedkar decided in 1956 to convert to Buddhism. It was an act of separatism, to be sure, but at the same time, it was also, as Ambedkar pointed out, affiliating with a religion that was far more universalist than Hinduism in its endorsement of social equality.[24] Ambedkar died only a few weeks after his conversion, only to be reborn some twenty years later as the prophet of Dalit liberation. That is his status today—a source of both realist wisdom and emancipatory dreams for India's oppressed castes.

To close my story about the unresolved conflict between universal affiliations and particular identities at the founding moment of democratic nationhood in India, let me point out what is at stake here today. At a meeting in 2000 in an Indian research institute, after a distinguished panel of academics and policymakers had bemoaned the decline of universalist ideals and moral values in national life, a Dalit activist from the audience asked why it was the case that liberal and leftist intellectuals were so pessimistic about where history was moving at the turn of the millennium. As far as he could see, the latter half of the twentieth century had been the brightest period in the entire history of the Dalits, since they had got rid of the worst forms of untouchability, mobilized themselves politically as a community, and were now making strategic alliances with other oppressed groups in order to get a share of governmental power. All this could happen because the conditions of mass democracy had thrown open the bastions of caste privilege to attack from the representatives of oppressed groups organized into electoral majorities. The panelists were silenced by this impassioned intervention. I came away persuaded once more that it is morally illegitimate to uphold the universalist ideals of nationalism without simultaneously demanding that the politics spawned by governmentality be recognized as an equally legitimate part of the real time-space of the modern political life of the nation. Without it, governmental technologies will continue to proliferate and serve, much as they did in the colonial era, as manipulable instruments of class rule in a global capitalist order. By seeking to find real ethical spaces for their operation in heterogeneous time, the incipient resistances to that order may succeed in inventing new terms of political justice.

TWO

Populations and Political Society

I

The classic moment when the promises of enlightened modernity appeared to come together with the universal political aspirations of citizenship within the nation was, of course, the French Revolution. The moment has been celebrated and canonized in numerous ways in the last two hundred years, perhaps most succinctly in the formula, now almost universally acknowledged, of the identity of the people with the nation and, in turn, the identity of the nation with the state. There is no question that the legitimacy of the modern state is now clearly and firmly grounded in a concept of popular sovereignty. This is, of course, the basis of modern democratic politics, but the idea of popular sovereignty has an influence that is more universal than that of democracy. Even the most undemocratic of modern regimes must claim its legitimacy not from divine right or dynastic succession or the right of conquest but from the will of the people, however expressed. Autocrats, military dictatorships, one-party regimes—all rule, or so they must say, on behalf of the people.

The power of the idea of popular sovereignty and its influence on democratic and national movements in Europe and the Americas in the nineteenth century is well known. But the influence extended far wider than what is now known as the modern West. The consequences of Napoleon's expedition to Egypt in 1798 have been much discussed.[1] Further east, the prince Tipu Sultan, ruler of Mysore, then locked in a ferocious struggle with the English in southern India, opened negotiations with the revolutionary government in France in 1797, of-

fering a treaty of alliance and friendship "founded on Republican
principles of sincerity and good faith, to the end that you and your
nation and myself and my people may become one family." It is said
that the prince was thrilled when he received a reply in which he was
addressed as "*Citoyen* Sultan Tipu."[2]

It is, of course, more than likely that Tipu's republican sympathies
went no deeper than his invocation, in his letter to "the gentlemen
of the Directory," of the tactical principle "that your enemies may be
mine and those of my people; and that my enemies may be considered
as yours." But no such reservations apply to the sentiments held by
the new generation of modernist reformers in nineteenth-century India. At school in Calcutta, we read of the historic voyage to England
in 1830 of Rammohun Roy, hailed as the father of Indian modernity.
When his boat stopped at Marseilles, we were told, Rammohun was
so eager to salute the tricolor, restored to its rightful place by the July
monarchy, that in hurrying down the gangway, he fell and broke his
leg. I discovered later from more reliable biographies that his injury
had occurred earlier, in Cape Town, but the infirmity could not
dampen his enthusiasm for liberty, equality, and fraternity. A fellow
passenger, I found out, wrote as follows: "Two French frigates, under
the revolutionary flag, the glorious tri-colour, were lying in Table Bay;
and lame as he was, he would insist on visiting them. The sight of
these colours seemed to kindle the flame of his enthusiasm, and to
render him insensible to pain." Rammohun was taken around the
vessels and he told his hosts "how much he was delighted to be under
the banner that waved over their decks—an evidence of the glorious
triumph of right over might; and as he left the vessels he repeated
emphatically 'Glory, glory, glory to France!' "[3]

On the other side of the globe, in the Caribbean, however, other
colonial people had in the meantime found out that there were limits
to the promise of universal citizenship, and they suffered more than
just a broken leg. The leaders of the Haitian revolution took seriously
the message of liberty and equality they heard from Paris and rose up
to declare the end of slavery. To their dismay, they were told by the
revolutionary government in France that the rights of man and citizen
did not extend to Negroes, even though they had declared themselves

free, because they were not, or not yet, citizens.[4] The great Mirabeau asked the National Assembly to remind the colonists that "in proportioning the number of deputies to the population of France, we have taken into consideration neither the number of our horses nor that of our mules."[5] In the end, after the Haitian revolutionaries declared their independence from colonial rule, the French sent an expeditionary force in 1802 to Saint-Domingue to reestablish colonial control as well as slavery. The historian Michel-Rolph Trouillot has said that the Haitian revolution occurred before its time. The entire spectrum of Western discourse in the age of Enlightenment had no place for black slaves claiming self-government by taking up arms: the idea was simply unthinkable.[6]

Thus, while creole nationalisms succeeded in proclaiming independent republics in Spanish America in the early nineteenth century, this was denied to the black Jacobins of Saint-Domingue. The world would have to wait for a century and a half before the rights of man and citizen would be allowed to extend that far. By then, however, with the success of democratic and national struggles all over the world, the constraints of class, rank, gender, race, caste, etc. would be gradually lifted from the idea of popular sovereignty, and universal citizenship would be recognized, as it now is, in the general right of self-determination of nations. Along with the modern state, the concept of the people and a discourse of rights have now become generalized within the idea of the nation. But a gulf has also been produced between the advanced democratic nations of the West and the rest of the world.

The modern form of the nation is both universal and particular. The universal dimension is represented, first, by the idea of the people as the original locus of sovereignty in the modern state, and second, by the idea of all humans as bearers of rights. If this was universally true, how was it to be realized? By enshrining the specific rights of *citizens* in a state constituted by a particular people, namely, a *nation.* Thus, the nation-state became the particular, and normal, form of the modern state. The basic framework of rights in the modern state was defined by the twin ideas of freedom and equality. But freedom and equality frequently pulled in opposite directions. The two, therefore, had to be mediated, as Étienne Balibar has usefully pointed out, by two further concepts: those of property and community.[7] *Property* sought to resolve the contradictions between freedom and equality at the level of the individual in relation to other individuals. *Community* was where the contradictions were sought to be resolved at the level of the whole fraternity. Along the dimension of property, the particular resolutions might be more or less liberal; along the dimension of community, they might be more or less communitarian. But it was within the specific form of the sovereign and homogeneous nation-state that the universal ideals of modern citizenship were expected to be realized.

Using theoretical shorthand, we could say that property and community defined the conceptual parameters within which the political discourse of capital, proclaiming liberty and equality, could flourish. The ideas of freedom and equality that gave shape to the universal rights of the citizen were crucial not only for the fight against absolutist political regimes but also for undermining pre-capitalist practices that restricted individual mobility and choice to traditional confines defined by birth and status. But they were also crucial, as the young Karl Marx noted, in separating the abstract domain of Right from the actual domain of life in civil society.[8] In legal-political theory, the rights of the citizen were unrestricted by race, religion, ethnicity, or class (by the early twentieth century, the same rights would also be made available to women), but this did not mean the abolition of actual distinctions between men (and women) in civil society. Rather, the universalism of the theory of rights both presupposed and enabled a new ordering of power relations in society based precisely on those distinctions of class, race, religion, gender, etc. At the same time, the emancipatory promise held out by the idea of universal equal rights also acted as a constant source of theoretical critique of actual civil society. That promise has, in the last two centuries, propelled numerous struggles all over the world to change unequal and unjust social differences of race, religion, caste, class, or gender.

Marxists have, in general, believed that the sway of capital over traditional community was the inevitable sign of historical progress. True, there is a deep sense of ambiguity in this judgment. If community was the social form of the unity of labor with the means of labor, then the destruction of that unity caused by the so-called primitive accumulation of capital produced a new laborer who was free not just to sell his labor as a commodity but free from all encumbrances of property except his labor-power. Marx wrote with bitter irony about this "double freedom" of the wage-laborer freed from the ties of pre-capitalist community.[9] But in 1853, he wrote of British rule in India as accomplishing a necessary social revolution: "whatever may have been the crimes of England," he wrote, "she was the unconscious tool of history in bringing about that revolution in India."[10] Late in his life, we know, he became far more skeptical of the revolutionary effects of colonial rule in agrarian societies like India and even speculated on the possibility of the Russian peasant community moving directly to a socialist form of collective life without going through the destructive phase of a capitalist transition.[11] Despite the lingering skepticism and irony, however, Marxists of the twentieth century generally welcomed the undermining of pre-capitalist property and the creation of large homogeneous political units such as nation-states. Where capital was seen to be performing the historical task of transition to more developed and modern forms of social production, it received the considered, albeit grudging and ambivalent, approval of Marxist historical theory.

When talking of equality, freedom, property and community in relation to the modern state, we are indeed talking of the political history of capital. The recent debate in Anglo-American political philosophy between liberals and communitarians seems to me to have confirmed the crucial role in this political history of the two mediating concepts of property and community in determining the range of institutional possibilities within the field constituted by freedom and equality. The communitarians could not reject the value of personal freedom, for if they overemphasized the claims of communal identity, they were open to the charge of denying the basic individual right to choose, possess, use and exchange commodities at will. On the other hand, liberals too did not deny that identifying with the community might be an important source of moral meaning for individual lives. Their concern was that by undermining the liberal system of rights and the liberal policy of neutrality on questions of the common good, communitarians were opening the door to majoritarian intolerance, the perpetuation of conservative practices, and a potentially tyrannical insistence on conformism. Few denied the empirical fact that most individuals, even in industrially advanced liberal democracies, led their lives within an inherited network of social attachments that could be described as community. But there was a strong feeling that not all communities were worthy of approval in modern political life. In particular, attachments that seemed to emphasize the inherited, the primordial, the parochial, or the traditional were regarded by most theorists as smacking of conservative and intolerant practices and hence as inimical to the values of modern citizenship. The political community that seemed to find the largest measure of approval was the modern nation that grants equality and freedom to all citizens irrespective of biological or cultural difference.[12]

This zone of legitimate political discourse, defined by the parameters of property and community, is emphasized even further by the new philosophical doctrine that calls itself republicanism and that claims to supersede the liberal-communitarian debate. Following upon the historical researches of John Pocock, this doctrine has been advanced most eloquently by Quentin Skinner and Philip Pettit.[13] Instead of the usual liberal understanding of freedom as negative liberty, i.e. the individual's freedom from interference, the aim of republicanism is to invoke the moment of anti-absolutism and claim that freedom is freedom from domination. This goal would urge the lover of freedom to fight, unlike what liberals would advocate, against all forms of domination, even when they are benign and do not normally involve interference. It would also allow the lover of freedom to support forms of interference that do not amount to domination. Thus, the republican would be in favor of governmental measures to ensure greater equality or to pursue the moral values of community as long as they do not imply an arbitrary power of domination. In this way, the theorists of republicanism argue, both the unattractiveness of a narrowly limited regime of liberal noninterference and the dangers of rampant communitarian populism can be avoided. The structures of property would not be threatened, while community in its sanitized and palatable forms could flourish.

I do not here wish to enter into the question of whether the republican claim actually leads to conclusions that are substantively different from those of the liberal theory of government. Instead, I would like to turn our attention to the institutional presuppositions that the doctrine of republicanism shares with that of liberalism. Whether individualist or communitarian or republican, all agree that their desired political institutions cannot be made to work effectively merely by legislating them into existence. They must, as Philip Pettit puts it rather cutely, "win a place in the habits of people's hearts."[14] They must, in other words, be nested in a network of norms in civil society that prevail independently of the state and that are consistent with its laws. Only such a civil society would provide, to use an old phraseology, the social base for capitalist democracy.

This was the grand theme of virtually all sociological theory in Europe in the nineteenth century. In the twentieth century, when the problem was posed of the possibility of capitalist transition in the non-Western world, the same presupposition provided the foundation for modernization theory, whether in its Marxian or Weberian version. The argument, to put it simply, was that without a transformation of the institutions and practices of civil society, whether carried out from the top or from below, it was impossible to create or sustain freedom and equality in the political domain. To have modern and free political communities, one must first have people who were citizens, not subjects. While no one would use any more the stark similes of eighteenth-century liberals, it was understood that horses and mules would not be able to represent themselves in government. For many, this understanding provided the ethical core of a project of modernization of the non-Western world: to transform erstwhile subjects, unfamiliar with the possibilities of equality and freedom, into modern citizens. In the previous chapter I described the dreams and frustrations of one such modernizer, B. R. Ambedkar.

II

However, while philosophical discussions on the rights of citizens in the modern state hovered around the concepts of liberty and community, the emergence of mass democracies in the advanced industrial countries of the West in the twentieth century produced an entirely new distinction—one between citizens and populations. Citizens inhabit the domain of theory, populations the domain of policy. Unlike the concept of citizen, the concept of population is wholly descriptive and empirical; it does not carry a normative burden. Populations are identifiable, classifiable, and describable by empirical or behavioral criteria and are amenable to statistical techniques such as censuses and sample surveys. Unlike the concept of citizen, which carries the ethical connotation of participation in the sovereignty of the state, the concept of population makes available to government functionaries a set of rationally manipulable instruments for reaching large sections of the inhabitants of a country as the targets of their "policies"—economic policy, administrative policy, law, and even political mobilization. Indeed, as Michel Foucault has pointed out, a major characteristic of the contemporary regime of power is a certain "governmentalization of the state."[15] This regime secures legitimacy not by the participation of citizens in matters of state but by claiming to provide for the well-being of the population. Its mode of reasoning is not deliberative openness but rather an instrumental notion of costs and benefits. Its apparatus is not the republican assembly but an elaborate network of surveillance through which information is collected on every aspect of the life of the population that is to be looked after.

It is not surprising that in the course of the twentieth century, ideas of participatory citizenship that were so much a part of the Enlightenment notion of politics have fast retreated before the triumphant advance of governmental technologies that have promised to deliver more well-being to more people at less cost. Indeed, one might say that the actual political history of capital has long spilled over the normative confines of liberal political theory to go out and conquer the world through its governmental technologies. Much of the emotional charge of the communitarian or republican critique of contemporary Western political life seems to flow from an awareness that the business of government has been emptied of all serious engagement with politics. This is shown most obviously in the steady fall in electoral participation in all Western democracies and even in the recent panic in left-liberal circles in Europe at the unexpected electoral success of right-wing populists.

How did the enumeration and classification of population groups for the purposes of welfare administration have this effect on the process of democratic politics in advanced capitalist countries? Many writers working in vastly diverse fields have thrown light on this question in recent years, from the philosopher Ian Hacking to the literary historian Mary Poovey.[16] Most relevant for us is the account given by British sociologists such as Nikolas Rose, Peter Miller, or Thomas Osborne of the actual working of governmentality in Britain and the United States.[17] They have surveyed the emergence of what has been called "government from the social point of view," typically in the areas of work, education, and health, in the nineteenth and twentieth centuries. There was, for instance, the rise of social insurance systems to minimize the uncertain impact of the economy on various groups and individuals. There was the constitution of the family itself, the subject of numerous pedagogical, medical, economic, and ethical discourses, as a site of governmentality. There was a proliferation of censuses and demographic surveys, making the work of governmentality accountable in terms of numbers, and leading in turn to the idea of representation by numerical proportions. The management of migration, crime, war and disease made personal identity itself an issue of security and therefore subject to record and constant verification. (The issue has suddenly loomed large in the United States and Britain in the wake of the recent panic over terrorism, and yet both countries have had for decades a plethora of agencies, both state and non-state, recording, verifying and validating the biological, social, and cultural details of personal identity.) All of this made governance less a matter of politics and more of administrative policy, a business for experts rather than for political representatives. Moreover, while the political fraternity of citizens had to be constantly affirmed as one and indivisible, there was no one entity of the governed. There was always a multiplicity of population groups that were the objects of governmentality—multiple targets with multiple characteristics, requiring multiple techniques of administration.

In short, the classical idea of popular sovereignty, expressed in the legal-political facts of equal citizenship, produced the homogeneous construct of the nation, whereas the activities of governmentality required multiple, cross-cutting and shifting classifications of the population as the targets of multiple policies, producing a necessarily heterogeneous construct of the social. Here, then, we have the antinomy between the lofty political imaginary of popular sovereignty and the mundane administrative reality of governmentality: it is the antinomy between the homogeneous national and the heterogeneous social. I might note in passing that when T. H. Marshall made his classic summation in 1949 of the story of the expansion of citizenship from civic to political to social rights, he was guilty of what we can now see was a category confusion. Applauding the progress of the welfare state in Britain, Marshall thought he was seeing the onward march of popular sovereignty and equal citizenship. In fact, it was an unprecedented proliferation of governmentality leading to the emergence of an intricately heterogeneous social.[18]

But in the chronological plotting of his story, Marshall was not wrong. The story of citizenship in the modern West moves from the institution of civic rights in civil society to political rights in the fully developed nation-state. Only then does one enter the relatively recent phase where "government from the social point of view" seems to take over. In countries of Asia and Africa, however, the chronological sequence is quite different. There the career of the modern state has been foreshortened. Technologies of governmentality often predate the nation-state, especially where there has been a relatively long experience of European colonial rule. In South Asia, for instance, the classification, description and enumeration of population groups as the objects of policy relating to land settlement, revenue, recruitment to the army, crime prevention, public health, management of famines and droughts, regulation of religious places, public morality, education, and a host of other governmental functions has a history of at least a century and a half before the independent nation-states of India, Pakistan, and Ceylon were born. The colonial state was what Nicholas Dirks has called an "ethnographic state."[19] Populations there had the status of subjects, not citizens. Obviously, colonial rule did not recognize popular sovereignty.

That was a concept that fired the imaginations of nationalist revolutionaries. Ideas of republican citizenship often accompanied the politics of national liberation. But without exception—and this is crucial for our story about politics in most of the world—they were overtaken by the developmental state which promised to end poverty and backwardness by adopting appropriate policies of economic growth and social reform. With varying degrees of success, and in some cases with disastrous failure, the postcolonial states deployed the latest governmental technologies to promote the well-being of their populations, often prompted and aided by international and nongovernmental organizations. In adopting these technical strategies of modernization and development, older ethnographic concepts often entered the field of knowledge about populations—as convenient descriptive categories for classifying groups of people into suitable targets for administrative, legal, economic, or electoral policy. In many cases, classificatory criteria used by colonial governmental regimes continued into the postcolonial era, shaping the forms of both political demands and developmental policy. Thus, caste and religion in India, ethnic groups in Southeast Asia, and tribes in Africa remained the dominant criteria for identifying communities among the populations as objects of policy. So much so that a huge ethnographic survey, recently undertaken by a governmental agency in India and published in 43 volumes, has actually claimed to have identified and described a total of exactly 4,635 communities that are supposed to constitute the population of India.[20]

We have therefore described two sets of conceptual connections. One is the line connecting civil society to the nation-state founded on popular sovereignty and granting equal rights to citizens. The other is the line connecting populations to governmental agencies pursuing multiple policies of security and welfare. The first line points to a domain of politics described in great detail in democratic political theory in the last two centuries. Does the second line point to a different domain of politics? I believe it does. To distinguish it from the classic associational forms of civil society, I am calling it *political society*.

In a series of recent papers, I have attempted to sketch out this conceptual field in the context of democratic politics in India.[21] I have favored retaining the old idea of civil society as bourgeois society, in the sense used by Hegel and Marx, and of using it in the Indian context as an actually existing arena of institutions and practices inhabited by a relatively small section of the people whose social locations can be identified with a fair degree of clarity. In terms of the *formal* structure of the state as given by the constitution and the laws, all of society is civil society; everyone is a citizen with equal rights and therefore to be regarded as a member of civil society. The political process is one where the organs of the state interact with members of civil society in their individual capacities or as members of associations.

This is, however, not how things work. Most of the inhabitants of India are only tenuously, and even then ambiguously and contextually, rights-bearing citizens in the sense imagined by the constitution. They are not, therefore, proper members of civil society and are not regarded as such by the institutions of the state. But it is not as though they are outside the reach of the state or even excluded from the domain of politics. As populations within the territorial jurisdiction of the state, they have to be both looked after and controlled by various governmental agencies. These activities bring these populations into a certain *political* relationship with the state. But this relationship does not always conform to what is envisaged in the constitutional depiction of the relation between the state and members of civil society. Yet these are without doubt political relations that may have acquired, in specific historically defined contexts, a widely recognized systematic character, and perhaps even certain conventionally recognized ethical norms, even if subject to varying degrees of contestation. How are we to begin to understand these processes?

Faced with similar problems, some analysts have favored expanding the idea of civil society to include virtually all existing social institutions that lie outside the strict domain of the state.[22] This practice has become rampant in the recent rhetoric of international financial institutions, aid agencies and nongovernmental organizations among whom the spread of a neoliberal ideology has authorized the consecration of every non-state organization as the precious flower of the associative endeavors of free members of civil society. I have preferred to resist these unscrupulously charitable theoretical gestures, principally because I feel it important not to lose sight of the vital and continually active project that still informs many of the state institutions in countries like India to transform traditional social authorities and practices into the modular forms of bourgeois civil society. Civil society as an *ideal* continues to energize an interventionist political project, but as an *actually existing form* it is demographically limited. Both of these facts must be borne in mind when considering the relation between modernity and democracy in countries such as India.

Some of you may recall a framework used in the early phase of the Subaltern Studies project in which we talked about a split in the domain of politics between an organized elite domain and an unorganized subaltern domain.[23] The idea of the split, of course, was intended to mark a fault line in the arena of nationalist politics in the three decades before independence during which the Indian masses, especially the peasantry, were drawn into organized political movements and yet remained distanced from the evolving forms of the postcolonial state. To say that there was a split in the domain of politics was to reject the notion, common to both liberal and Marxist historiographies, that the peasantry lived in some "pre-political" stage of collective action. It was to say that peasants in their collective actions were also being political, except that they were political in a way different from that of the elite. Since those early experiences of the imbrication of elite and subaltern politics in the context of the anticolonial movements, the democratic process in India has come a long way in bringing under its influence the lives of the subaltern classes. It is to understand these relatively recent forms of the entanglement of elite and subaltern politics that I am proposing the notion of a *political society.*

In illustrating what I mean by political society and how it works, I will describe in the next chapter several cases studied in recent field work where we can see a politics emerging out of the developmental policies of government aimed at specific population groups. Many of these groups, organized into associations, transgress the strict lines of legality in struggling to live and work. They may live in illegal squatter settlements, make illegal use of water or electricity, travel without tickets in public transport. In dealing with them, the authorities cannot treat them on the same footing as other civic associations following more legitimate social pursuits. Yet state agencies and nongovernmental organizations cannot ignore them either, since they are among thousands of similar associations representing groups of population whose very livelihood or habitation involve violation of the law. These agencies therefore deal with these associations not as bodies of citizens but as convenient instruments for the administration of welfare to marginal and underprivileged population groups.

These groups on their part accept that their activities are often illegal and contrary to good civic behavior, but they make a claim to a habitation and a livelihood as a matter of right. They profess a readiness to move out if they are given suitable alternative sites for resettlement, for instance. The state agencies recognize that these population groups do have some claim on the welfare programs of the government, but those claims could not be regarded as justiciable rights since the state did not have the means to deliver those benefits to the entire population of the country. To treat those claims as rights would only invite further violation of public property and civic laws.

What happens then is a negotiation of these claims on a political terrain where, on the one hand, governmental agencies have a public obligation to look after the poor and the underprivileged and, on the other, particular population groups receive attention from those agencies according to calculations of political expediency. Groups in political society have to pick their way through this uncertain terrain by making a large array of connections outside the group—with other groups in similar situations, with more privileged and influential groups, with government functionaries, perhaps with political parties and leaders. They often make instrumental use of the fact that they can vote in elections, so that it is true to say that the field of citizenship, at certain points, overlaps with that of governmentality. But the instrumental use of the vote is possible only within a field of strategic politics. This is the stuff of democratic politics as it takes place on the ground in India. It involves what appears to be a constantly shifting compromise between the normative values of modernity and the moral assertion of popular demands.

Civil society then, restricted to a small section of culturally equipped citizens, represents in countries like India the high ground of modernity. So does the constitutional model of the state. But in actual practice, governmental agencies must descend from that high ground to the terrain of political society in order to renew their legitimacy as providers of well-being and there to confront whatever is the current configuration of politically mobilized demands. In the process, one is liable to hear complaints from the protagonists of civil society and the constitutional state that modernity is facing an unexpected rival in the form of democracy.

I now turn to the very different, and often contradictory, political significance of civil society and political society. Let me do this by giving you one more story from the domain of popular politics in the Indian city.[24]

III

On May 5, 1993, in the early hours of dawn, a man died in a Calcutta hospital. He had been admitted a few days before and was being treated for diabetes, renal failure and cerebro-vascular accident. His condition had deteriorated rapidly in the previous twenty-four hours and, although the doctors attending him struggled through the night, their efforts were in vain. A senior doctor of the hospital signed the death certificate.

The name of the man who died was Birendra Chakrabarti, but he was better known as Balak Brahmachari, leader of the Santan Dal, a religious sect with a large following in the southern and central districts of West Bengal. The sect itself is no more than fifty years old, although it probably has its antecedents in earlier sectarian movements among the lower-caste, especially Namasudra, peasants of central Bengal. Its religious doctrines are highly eclectic, consisting entirely of the views of Balak Brahmachari himself as expressed in his sayings, but they are characterized in particular by a curious involvement in political matters. The sect's mouthpiece *Kara Chabuk* [The Strong Whip] regularly published its leader's comments on current political subjects in which there was the recurrent theme of "revolution," a cataclysmic churning that would surgically cleanse a corrupt and putrid social order. The sect, in fact, first came into the public spotlight in the period 1967–1971 when it participated in political demonstrations in support of the Left parties and against Congress rule. The Santan Dal activists, with many women in their ranks, some in saffron clothes, holding aloft their tridents and shouting their slogan "Ram Narayan Ram," were an incongruous element in Leftist demonstrations in Calcutta at the time, and could not but attract attention. But no one accused the sect of opportunistic political ambitions, because it made no claims to electoral representation or recognition as a political party. Since then, many of the followers of the sect have been known to be sympathizers and even activists of the Left, especially of the Communist Party of India (Marxist), leading partner in the Left Front which has ruled West Bengal continuously since 1977.

On this particular morning in May 1993, the followers of Balak Brahmachari refused to accept that their spiritual leader was dead. They recalled that several years ago, in 1967, he had gone into *samadhi* for twenty-two days during which, from all outward appearances, he was dead. But he had woken up from his trance and returned to normal life. Now once more, they said, their Baba had gone into *nirvikalpa samadhi*, a state of suspension of bodily functions that could be achieved only by those with the highest spiritual powers. The members of Santal Dal took the body of Balak Brahmachari from hospital to their ashram in Sukhchar, a northern suburb of Calcutta, and began to keep what they said would be a long vigil.

Soon the matter became a *cause célèbre* in Calcutta. The press picked it up, publishing reports of how the body was being kept on slabs of ice under heavy airconditioning. One Bengali daily, *Ajkal*, pursued the story with particular vigor, turning it into a fight for rational values in public life and against obscurantist beliefs and practices. It accused the local authorities and the health department of the West Bengal government of failing to implement their own rules regarding the disposal of dead bodies and of conniving in the making of a serious public hazard. Soon the authorities were forced to respond. On the thirteenth day of the vigil, the Panihati municipality made clear that it had served the Santal Dal leaders with a notice asking them to cremate the body immediately, but that under the municipal laws it had no powers to carry out a forcible cremation.[25] On behalf of the Santal Dal, Chitta Sikdar, the secretary, kept up a regular defensive campaign in the press, maintaining that the spiritual phenomenon of *nirvikalpa samadhi* was beyond the understanding of medical science and that Balak Brahmachari would soon resume his normal bodily life.

The standoff continued. *Ajkal* raised the tempo of its campaign, opening its columns to prominent intellectuals and public figures who deplored the persistence of such superstitious and unscientific beliefs among the people. Groups of activists from progressive cultural organizations, the popular science movement and the rationalist society began to hold demonstrations in front of the Santan Dal headquarters in Sukhchar. *Ajkal* spared no efforts to provoke the spokesmen of the Dal and to ridicule their statements, refusing to refer to the dead leader by his sectarian name of Balak Brahmachari and instead calling him "Balak Babu"—a nonsensical "Mr. Balak." There were some heated confrontations at the gate of the Santan Dal ashram, with the Dal activists reportedly stocking arms and preparing for a showdown. One night, some crackers and handmade bombs exploded outside the ashram and a group of Dal activists came out and shouted over their loudspeakers: "The revolution has begun."[26]

Nearly a month after the official death of Balak Brahmachari, his body still lay on ice slabs in an airconditioned room with his followers waiting for him to break his *samadhi. Ajkal* claimed that there was an unbearable stench in the entire neighborhood of Sukhchar and that the residents of the area had had enough. Now it began to be openly alleged that the government was reluctant to intervene because of politics. The elections to the local government bodies in rural West Bengal, the crucial panchayats which had become the backbone of Left Front support, were scheduled for the last week of May. Any action against the Dal could antagonize a lot of Left Front supporters in at least four districts of West Bengal. It was also suggested that some important leaders of the CPI(M) were sympathetic to the Santan Dal and that one minister in particular, Subhas Chakrabarti, minister in charge of tourism and sports, was regarded by Dal members as a fraternal supporter.

On June 25, 1993, fifty-one days after the official death of Balak Brahmachari, the health minister of West Bengal announced that a medical team consisting of leading specialists in medicine, neurology and forensic medicine would examine the body of Balak Brahmachari and submit a report to the government. The Indian Medical Association, the apex professional body of medical practitioners, immediately protested saying that to call for a new examination implied a lack of confidence in the death certificate issued from the hospital. It pointed out that no scientific grounds had been furnished to question the original judgment of the hospital doctors. The government doctors went ahead nevertheless and returned from Sukhchar to say that they had not been allowed to touch the body. They reported that the body had been putrefied and carried signs of mummification and that it had not decayed completely because of the extremely low temperature at which it had been kept.[27]

By this time, Subhas Chakrabarti had been given charge by the CPI(M) leadership to devise a solution to the impasse. Accompanied by the local CPI(M) leaders, he visited the Sukhchar ashram and later told journalists that he was trying to persuade the followers of the Baba to cremate the body. He agreed that there was no scientific reason for doctors to reexamine a body that had been certified as dead, but insisted that this was a necessary part of the process of persuasion. He pointed out that "Babadom" was still prevalent in the country and that thousands of people were followers of these religious leaders. He warned that it was dangerous to take religious fanaticism lightly. It was the government's view, he said, that applying force could provoke fanaticism. When asked if he was aware of the health hazard that had been created in the neighborhood of Sukhchar, he claimed that he had smelt nothing, but that was probably because he was a habitual inhaler of snuff.[28]

On June 30, in a four-hour operation beginning at two in the morning, a force consisting of 5,000 policemen stormed the Santan Dal headquarters, took charge of the body, and removed it to a nearby crematorium. *The Telegraph* reported that the last rites were performed by the guru's brother "as the security cordon pushed back wailing women who still believed their departed cult leader would be resurrected. The state government, severely criticised for soft-pedalling the issue, heaved a sigh of relief." The police force, which was attacked by Dal activists with acid bulbs, knives, tridents, glass bottles, and chilli powder, used tear gas shells to immobilize the defenders and blow-torches to make its way through window grilles and collapsible gates into the heavily fortified headquarters. But it did not resort to shooting. Many Dal activists as well as policemen were hurt, but, as the official press release put it, "there were no casualties."[29]

The minister Subhas Chakrabarti congratulated the police and the local administration for carrying out a very difficult and sensitive operation. He referred to the popular Hindi film *Jugnu* and said the job was more difficult than what the actor Dharmendra had faced in that film. "Of course," he said to journalists, "you think all that is lumpen culture, but I think it is an apt example." The following day, *Ajkal* in its editorial announced: "We have come to the end of that age in West Bengal when lumpen culture could be called lumpen culture. Progressive West Bengal has seen the end of the age of reason. Now begins the age of *Jugnu*."[30]

Despite the relatively smooth and successful conclusion of the matter, the controversy did not die down. Chitta Sikdar, the secretary of the Santan Dal, protested to the chief minister against what he described as an authoritarian and undemocratic action of the government. He said the treatment received by Balak Brahmachari at the hands of the rulers of society would be remembered in history in the same way as the trials of Jesus Christ, Galileo, and Socrates. On the other hand, opinions such as that of *Ajkal* condemned as opportunistic the attempt by sections of the government and the ruling party to target the second-rank leaders of the sect for misleading their innocent followers and profiting from their overexcited religious sentiments but not criticizing the sects and the so-called godmen themselves for spreading unreason and superstition. Twelve days after the cremation of Balak Brahmachari, the secretary of the Santan Dal and eighty-two others were arrested and charged with rioting, assault, obstruction of justice, and other offenses.[31]

Members of the Santan Dal continued for several months to write letters to newspapers portraying themselves as victims of an undemocratic and illegal police action. They asked what laws of the land the Baba's followers had broken by believing that he would come back to them. Did a religious belief in extraordinary spiritual powers deserve blows from the policeman's truncheon? And was it not the case that the Dal followers were finally subjected to police action because most of them were low-caste peasants whose marginal political value had evaporated after the local government elections were over? While public memory might be short, one letter warned, the memory of victimhood was merciless. The perpetrators of injustice would one day meet their day of judgment.[32]

The case illustrates, I think, several of the points I have raised so far about the relation between civil society and democracy in a country like India. A modern civil society, consistent with the ideas of freedom and equality, is a project that is located in the historical desires of certain elite sections of Indians. The specific story of the emergence and flowering of those desires and their sources in colonial projects has been much discussed. When the country was under colonial rule, these elites believed the crucial transformative processes that would change the traditional beliefs and practices of the people and fashion a new modern national self must be kept out of the reach of the colonial state apparatus. With the end of colonial rule and the coming to power of these classes in the postcolonial state, that transformative project became firmly located in the dynamic potential of the organs of the new national state. That those organs were now part of a constitutional system of representative democracy made the modernizing project an expression of the will of the people and thus gloriously consistent with the legitimizing norms of modernity itself.

Although many of the sites and activities characteristic of the arena I have called political society can be shown to have emerged within the spectrum of nationalist political mobilizations in the colonial period, I would say that it has taken on something like a distinct form only since the 1980s. Two conditions have facilitated this process.

One is the rise to dominance of a notion of governmental performance that emphasizes the welfare and protection of populations—the "pastoral" functions of government, as Michel Foucault called it—using similar governmental technologies all over the world but largely independent of considerations of active participation by citizens in the sovereignty of the state. This has enabled the mutual recognition by state agencies and population groups that governments are obliged to deliver certain benefits even to people who are not proper members of civil society or of the republican body of true citizens. If the nation-state cannot do this job, it must be done by nongovernmental—if necessary, international—agencies The second condition is the widening of the arena of political mobilization, prompted by electoral considerations and often only for electoral ends, from formally organized structures such as political parties with well-ordered internal constitutions and coherent doctrines and programs to loose and often transient mobilizations, building on communication structures that would not be ordinarily recognized as political (for instance, religious assemblies or cultural festivals, or more curiously, even associations of cinema fans, as in some of the southern Indian states).

The proliferation of activities in this arena of political society has caused much discomfort and apprehension in progressive elite circles in recent years. The comment about "lumpen culture" in the *Ajkal* editorial I cited earlier is typical. The complaint is widespread in middle-class circles today that politics has been taken over by mobs and criminals. The result is the abandonment—or so the complaint goes—of the mission of the modernizing state to change a backward society. Instead, what we see is the importation of the disorderly, corrupt, and irrational practices of unreformed popular culture into the very hallways and chambers of civic life, all because of the calculations of electoral expediency. The noble pursuit of modernity appears to have been seriously compromised because of the compulsions of parliamentary democracy.

Given a history in India of more than a hundred years of modern representative institutions, we can now see a pattern of evolution of this familiar Tocquevillian problem.[33] Early Indian liberals like Dadabhai Naoroji or Gopal Krishna Gokhale or even Mohammad Ali Jinnah in the early phase of his political life were entirely convinced of the inherent value of those institutions, but they were also hugely circumspect about the conditions in which those institutions could function. As good nineteenth-century liberals, they would have been the first to specify requirements such as education and a proved commitment to civic life that would have to be met before a people could be considered fit, in their language, "to receive parliamentary institutions." If we look at it from another angle, we might say that for men like Naoroji or Gokhale, democracy was a good form of government only when it could be adequately controlled by men of status and wisdom. With the rise of the so-called Extremists in nationalist politics, especially with the Khilafat and Noncooperation movements, there came into organized political life in India many forces and many ideas that did not care too much about the niceties of parliamentary politics. It was Gandhi, of course, who in this period, intervened decisively in the political arena created by the new representative institutions of the late colonial order. Even as he claimed to reject parliamentary institutions along with all of the other trappings of modern civilization, he was more instrumental than anyone else in bringing about the mobilization that would in the end make the Indian National Congress the ruling political organization of independent India. As has been shown in many studies, Gandhi's words and actions are shot through by the parallel themes of unleashing popular initiative and controlling it at the same time.[34] With the formalization of Congress rule in the first decade and a half after independence, control became the dominant motif in the close interweaving of state initiative and electoral approval in the so-called Congress system of the Nehru period.

The journey from the Nehru period to the crisis of the mid-1960s to the reestablishment of Congress dominance in the state populism of the first Indira Gandhi regime is a trajectory that is not unfamiliar to the historical experience of many third-world countries. What was distinctive in the life of Indian democracy is, I think, the defeat of Indira Gandhi's emergency regime in a parliamentary election. It brought about a decisive shift in all subsequent discussion about the essence and appearance of democracy, its form and content, its inner nature and outward appearance. Whatever may be the judgment of historians on the "real" causes of the collapse of the emergency regime, the 1977 elections established in the arena of popular mobilizations in India the capacity of the vote and of representative bodies of government to give voice to popular demands of a kind that had never before been allowed to disturb the order and tranquility of the proverbial corridors of power. One cannot but wonder if this is not the momentous experience that separates the popular understanding of democracy in India from that in neighboring Pakistan where it has been possible in recent times for both elites and subalterns to say in unison that electoral democracy is a fake and that the path to true democracy may have to pass through a spell of military dictatorship.

But lest we in India be too quick to congratulate ourselves, let me restate my argument. The contrary themes of popular legitimacy and elite control—the perennial problem of democratic theory itself as represented by the two mediating concepts of community and property—were embedded in the conception of Indian democracy from the very beginning. They have not gone away, nor have they been resolved or superseded. They have only taken new forms as a result of the ongoing struggles between elite and popular conceptions of democracy. They are being played out once again in the recent debates over democratic modernization in India. On the one hand, the uncertain demands of popular ratification have led committed modernizers to throw up their hands and lament that the age of reason had been brought to an end by the political surrender to the forces of disorder and irrationality. They read the many compromises with electoral compulsions as signs of the abandonment of enlightened politics. Generally less noticed are the transformative effects of these contrary mobilizations among the supposedly unenlightened sections of the population. Since this is an area that is only beginning to be studied, I can only make certain preliminary observations on it, and will do so in the next chapter. But this constitutes, I believe, the most profound and significant set of social changes that are being produced by the democratic process in countries like India today.

I should also note that one response to these social changes has already evolved among the governing classes in India. I see this as a variant of the colonial strategy of indirect rule. This involves a suspension of the modernization project, walling in the protected zones of bourgeois civil society and dispensing the governmental functions of law and order and welfare through the "natural leaders" of the governed populations. The strategy, in other words, seeks to preserve the civic virtues of bourgeois life from the potential excesses of electoral democracy.

The other response is less cynical, even as it is more pragmatic. It does not abandon the project of enlightenment, but attempts to steer it through the thicket of contestations in what I have called political society. It takes seriously the functions of direction and leadership of a vanguard, but accepts that the legal arm of the state in a country like India cannot reach into a vast range of social practices that continue to be regulated by other beliefs and administered by other authorities. But it also knows that those dark zones are being penetrated by the welfare functions of modern governmental practices, producing those effects on claims and representation that I have called the urge for democratization. This is the zone in which the project of democratic modernity has to operate—slowly, painfully, unsurely.

In bringing up the example of the negotiations over the disposal of a dead body in Calcutta, I was not trying to provide a narrative of the correct handling of contradictions among the people. Nor was I describing a case of successful governance. Nor am I saying that the specific form in which a local crisis of modernity-versus-democracy was resolved on that occasion flowed out of a conscious political project of social transformation in which the ruling parties in West Bengal are engaged. Rather, my intention was to point out the possibilities that exist in that normatively nebulous zone that I have called political society. When I use that term, I am always reminded that in the *Prison Notebooks*, Antonio Gramsci begins by equating political society with the state, but soon slides into a whole range of social and cultural interventions that must take place well beyond the domain of the state. It is clear that in pushing the project of turning subaltern subjects into national citizens, the modernizers have encountered resistances that are facilitated by the activities of political society. But I have tried to emphasize that even in resisting the modernizing project that is imposed on them, the subaltern classes also embark on a path of internal transformation. In the next chapter I provide some examples of this incipient process of change. At the same time, in carrying out their pedagogical mission in political society, the educators—enlightened people like us—might also succeed in educating themselves. That, I submit, would be the most enriching and historically significant result of the encounter between modernity and democracy in most of the world.

THREE

The Politics of the Governed

I

Let me take you on a quick tour through political society, or at least those parts of it that I am familiar with, because there are many parts about which I know very little.

Our first stop is along the railway tracks that run through the southern part of the city of Calcutta, not far from where I live and work. A major arterial road flies over the tracks. If you stand on the bridge and look in front of you, you will see high-rise apartment blocks, a ritzy shopping mall, and the offices of a major oil company. But if you look down, you will see a narrow line of shanties, with irregular tin or tile roofs lined with dirty plastic sheets, running all along and perilously close to the railway tracks. These belong to squatters who have been living here for more than fifty years. In the early 1990s, some of my colleagues at the Centre for Studies in Social Sciences, Calcutta, under the direction of Asok Sen, carried out a study of one section of these shanties.[1] This section has the official name of Gobindapur Rail Colony Gate Number 1 and contains a population of about 1,500 people.

The settlement apparently emerged in the late 1940s when a small group of peasants from southern Bengal, who had lost their lands in the aftermath of the great famine of 1943, came to the city in search of a livelihood. Soon there were thousands of others streaming into the city every day. These new migrants were from eastern Bengal, now East Pakistan. They were refugees produced by the partition of India. Over the next decade, the suburbs of Calcutta would accommodate a refugee immigration of more than three times the original population of the city. Most of them settled on public, and sometimes private, property—illegally, but with the tacit acquiescence of the authorities, because where else would they go? The refugee settlements acquired the official, and popular, name of "colonies."

The stories told by some of the early settlers of our railway colony make it seem almost like a frontier settlement. Four or five men took the lead in organizing the place. They invited in new settlers, divided up plots, helped build the huts and shacks. They also charged rents from the new settlers. Adhir Mandal and Haren Manna were the two key men in the colony until the mid-1970s.[2] They had made links with the Communist Party, the growing opposition political force with strong support among the refugee populations in the city. They dealt with the railway authorities, the police, and other government agencies on behalf of the colony. Adhir Mandal owned about two hundred shacks which he rented out and was known at this time as the *zamindar* of the rail colony—the landlord—such was his dominance. Communist Party leaders now say that Adhir and a few others were the "local vested interests" although they were with the party. "They behaved like bullies," one party leader said, "and were involved in petty graft and extortion. Adhir was very clever. . . . Haren Manna often stole a part of the funds he raised for the party. We overlooked these things since it was difficult to find a replacement for him. . . . How could we expect to find in the rail colony an honest person with Haren's drive and initiative?"

From time to time the railway authorities would make attempts to remove the squatters and reclaim the land. In 1965, the railway engineers tried to build a wall to encircle the settlement. The residents set up a human wall, with women in the front, preventing the trucks carrying the building materials from coming near the colony. During the emergency in 1975, there was a serious threat of eviction. Some nearby settlements were razed to the ground by bulldozers. Our rail colony residents mobilized a member of the state assembly from the pro-Soviet Communist Party, then allied with Indira Gandhi's ruling Congress Party, to intercede with the chief minister and dissuade the railway authorities from carrying out the demolition. The threat passed.

What we have said so far will not be unfamiliar to those who have read or heard about political mobilization within the electoral system inaugurated in postcolonial India. There are hundreds of similar stories that have come from the cities and villages of India. They were generally summarized under a theory of patron-client relationships, of vote banks, of faction leaders. One distinct feature of our case might have been the involvement of the cadre-based, deeply ideological, Communist Party, but even that, as we saw from the interview with the party leader, was not, at least in this case, very much more than a mutual arrangement of convenience. The party made no claims that Adhir Mandal or Haren Manna were communist revolutionaries mobilizing the people for political action. This was not political society as I have described it.

A new trend, however, emerged from the early 1980s. Adhir Mandal, the so-called *zamindar*, was now dead. In 1983, the railways again attempted to put a fence around the settlement. The residents organized once more to resist the move. They had a new leader now, a somewhat unlikely character named Anadi Bera. He was called the Master, because he ran a primary school across the street from the rail colony. Although lacking a high school education Bera taught the poor children of the area to read and write. His real popularity, however, was as a theatre enthusiast. He organized and acted in amateur *jatra* performances, the open air theatre-in-the-round form so popular in Bengal. It was through his theatrical activities that he came in touch with the residents of the rail colony. He had his own problems with accommodation, and soon he rented a shack in the colony and moved in.

Anadi Bera was the chief organizer of the resistance by the squatters in 1983. In 1986, he set up a new association of the residents of the colony—Jana Kalyan Samiti, the People's Welfare Association—with the objective of starting a medical center and a library. The local municipal officials, political party leaders, officers of the local police station, and prominent middle-class residents of the neighboring apartment blocks were regularly approached to raise funds for the association or to be involved with its activities. The government had started a major health and literacy program for children in urban slums called the Integrated Child Development Scheme (ICDS). At Anadi Bera's initiative, the ICDS opened a child-care unit at the rail colony. The unit was located in the association's office room. The ICDS immunizes children against polio, tuberculosis, tetanus, and other diseases, provides them with a daily snack, and has a trained staff to run a play school and to provide counseling to parents on birth control options. The ICDS staff also maintains a detailed record of the livelihoods, income, consumption, and health of every family in the colony.

The ICDS scheme is one example of how the residents of our squatters' colony could organize to get themselves identified as a distinct population group that could receive the benefits of a governmental program. But that is not the only instance. Having set up the association, the residents now use this collective form to deal with other governmental agencies such as the railways, the police or municipal authorities, with NGOs offering welfare or developmental services, and with political parties and leaders. For instance, if one inquired about how the colony got electricity, since electric fans and television sets are not uncommon appliances in the shacks, the residents are usually evasive. At least, that is how it was at the time of Professor Asok Sen's fieldwork. One suspected then that electric wires were illegally tapped. But there are many stories from Indian cities where electric companies, faced with the persistent theft of electricity and the legal difficulty of recognizing illegal squatters as legitimate individual consumers, have negotiated collective rental arrangements with entire squatter settlements represented precisely through associations of the kind we have described. There is thus an entire set of paralegal arrangements that can grow in order to deliver civic services and welfare benefits to population groups whose very habitation or livelihood lies on the other side of legality. I later found out that sometime in the late 1980s, the colony actually did obtain a legal electricity connection through six community meters organized by their Welfare Association. Not only that, since 1996, the residents even have individual electrical connections. The municipal authority also supplies them with water and public toilet facilities. All of this, of course, on illegally occupied public land barely a yard or two away from the railway lines. But I am getting ahead of my story.

Although the crucial move here was for our squatters to seek and find recognition as a population group, which from the standpoint of governmentality is only a usable empirical category that defines the targets of policy, they themselves have had to find ways of investing their collective identity with a moral content. This is an equally crucial part of the politics of the governed: *to give to the empirical form of a population group the moral attributes of a community.* In the case of our rail colony, there was no pre-given communal form readily available to them. Some of the residents came from southern Bengal, others from the former East Pakistan, now Bangladesh. Most of them belong to different middle and low castes, although there is a sprinkling of upper castes too. A survey carried out in the mid-1990s found that 56 percent of the residents belonged to the Scheduled Castes, the legally recognized category of former untouchable castes that are entitled to affirmative benefits from the government, and 4 percent to the Scheduled Tribes; the rest are other Hindu castes.[3]

The community, such as it exists here, was built from scratch. When the leading members of the association speak about the colony and its struggles, they do not talk of the shared interests of the members of an association. Rather, they describe the community in the more compelling terms of a shared kinship. The most common metaphor they use is that of the family. "We are all a single family," said Ashu Das, an active member of the association. "We don't distinguish between refugees from East Bengal and those from villages in West Bengal. We have no other place to build our homes. We have collectively occupied this land for so many years. This is the basis for our claim to our own homes."

Badal Das, another resident, explains why they have to stick together as a family. "We live in the face of the tiger," he said, using a saying that is common in southern Bengal, where tigers and humans have long lived as adversaries, to refer figuratively to the ever-present threat of eviction. But it is not any prior biological or even cultural affinity that defines this family. Rather, it is the collective occupation of a piece of land—a territory clearly defined in time and space and one that is under threat.

It is remarkable how clearly the residents define the limits of their so-called family: they are defined by the territorial limits of the "colony." Ashu Das explained: "The other side of the bridge is another neighborhood. That area should be left to the men of that neighborhood. We don't cross the limits." Those limits are often crucial in determining claims: who can become members of the association, who must contribute to collective festivities, or who can demand jobs as security guards in the middle-class apartment blocks in the neighborhood.

Within the so-called family, now, there is much internal variety. Few men have specialized skills or stable jobs: most go out looking for temporary jobs as laborers in the construction business. The women usually work as domestic help in neighboring middle-class houses and are often the principal earners in their households. In the early 1990s, when this study was carried out, the earnings of the colony residents varied from Rs.1,000 ($30) to below Rs.100 ($3) per month per capita. A different survey carried out a few years later found that more than half the families had total earnings of less than Rs.2,000 per month, the average income of the settlement being less than Rs.500 per capita per month. Some were owners of shacks rented out to other residents—all outside the pale of the law, of course, because no one had any legal title—but there appeared to be little conflict here between landlords and tenants.

Most disputes between neighbors and even between marital partners were settled by the Welfare Association. Not everyone was happy with this intrusiveness. One woman who had moved into the colony after her marriage said that she found her neighbors too nosey and given to backbiting. But community life was also sustained by sports activities, collective viewing of television shows and videos, and by religious festivals. The biggest festival organized by the association is the annual worship of the goddess Sitala. She has a curious history, originating in rural south Bengal as a folk goddess dispensing or preventing the spread of smallpox. In recent years, now that smallpox has been eradicated, she has emerged in the slums of Calcutta as a goddess who generally looks after the health of her children. She is now worshipped in week-long festivals, financed by small donations from slum residents, in defiant imitation of the middle-class festival of the much better known and infinitely more glamorous Brahminical goddess Durga. During the Sitala festival, the association organizes musical shows and *jatra* performances, their "master" Anadi Bera naturally taking a leading role. A lesser festival is the worship of the goddess Kali where the younger men of the colony are given a free rein, with video shows, meat-eating and drinking.

The People's Welfare Association created by the residents of Rail Colony Gate Number One is not an association of civil society. It springs from a collective violation of property laws and civic regulations. The state cannot recognize it as having the same legitimacy as other civic associations pursuing more legitimate objectives. The squatters, on their part, admit that their occupation of public land is both illegal and contrary to good civic life. But they make a claim to a habitation and a livelihood as a matter of right and use their association as the principal collective instrument to pursue that claim. In one of its petitions to the railway authorities, the association wrote:

> Among us are refugees from erstwhile East Pakistan and landless people from South Bengal. Having lost everything—means of livelihood, land and even homestead, we had to come to Calcutta to eke out a living and in search of shelter. . . . we are mostly day labourers and household help, living below the poverty line. We have somehow built a shelter of our own. If our homes are broken and we are evicted from the shanties, we have nowhere to go.

Refugees, landless people, day laborers, homestead, below the poverty line—are all demographic categories of governmentality. That is the ground on which they define their claims. In the same petition, the association also states that "along with other citizens of Calcutta," it is in favor of the improvement and extension of the city's railway services. If, for this purpose, it was "absolutely necessary to shift us from our present dwellings," the association demanded a "suitable alternative homestead." Thus, alongside its reference to the government's obligation to look after poor and underprivileged population groups, the association was also appealing to the moral rhetoric of a community striving to build a decent social life under extremely harsh conditions and, at the same time, affirming the duties of good citizenship. The categories of governmentality were being invested with the imaginative possibilities of community, including its capacity to invent relations of kinship, to produce a new, even if somewhat hesitant, rhetoric of political claims.

These claims are irreducibly political. They could only be made on a political terrain, where rules may be bent or stretched, and not on the terrain of established law or administrative procedure. The success of these claims depends entirely on the ability of particular population groups to mobilize support to influence the implementation of governmental policy in their favor. But this success is necessarily temporary and contextual. The strategic balance of political forces could change and rules may no longer be bent as before. As I have pointed out, governmentality always operates on a heterogeneous social field, on multiple population groups, and with multiple strategies. Here there is no equal and uniform exercise of the rights of citizenship.

Thus, it is quite possible for the equilibrium of strategic politics to shift enough for these squatters to be evicted tomorrow. (In fact, in early 2002, after these lectures were delivered, a citizens' group successfully moved a public interest litigation in the Calcutta High Court demanding the eviction of the settlers in the rail colony because they were polluting the waters of the Rabindra Sarobar lake in south Calcutta. A substantial section of the squatters had, in the meantime, shifted their allegiance from the Left Front to the Trinamul Congress. In early March, they managed to physically beat back a police force sent in by the government to implement the court order. They are now hoping against hope that their party leader would soon be reinstated as Railway Minister in the Union government in New Delhi; they might then get rehabilitation before they are forcibly evicted. Such is the tenuous logic of strategic politics in political society.)

To illustrate how a shift in the strategic balance of political forces can dramatically affect the lives of thousands of people surviving on the margins of urban life, let us walk up the avenue about half a mile to the north of the railway tracks. This is Gariahat, the heart of middle-class south Calcutta. They are now building a new fly-over at the busy crossing here. A year or so ago, these were wide avenues, with broad sidewalks and brightly lit shop-fronts. Middle-class residents were happy that their city was being restored to its original beauty and charm, before the streets and sidewalks had been taken over by thousands of street vendors. For almost thirty years since the mid-1960s, the major roads of the city were clogged with rows of shabby kiosks, occupying most of the sidewalks and frequently spilling on to the roadway itself. The pavement stalls were clearly performing an important economic function and providing a low-level but vital source of livelihood to thousands of people. The vendors had operated strategically in political society, successfully mobilizing support among citizens and political parties to establish and maintain their tenuous, and clearly illegal, occupation of the streets. In the mid-1990s, however, the tide turned. There was increasing pressure on the communist-led government of West Bengal to clean up Calcutta in order to attract foreign investment in growth sectors such as petrochemicals and electronics. The government's support among the urban middle classes was falling sharply. In 1996, Subhas Chakrabarti, the minister who had successfully organized the disposal of Balak Brahmachari's dead body, was given charge of clearing the Calcutta streets. Over a period of two weeks, in a well-planned coordinated action codenamed Operation Sunshine, municipal authorities and the police demolished all street-side stalls in Calcutta, cleared the sidewalks, expanded the roadways and planted trees. The vendors were still organized. Sensing that they were being abandoned by the Left, they now turned to the opposition parties. They did not resist physically; there were no violent confrontations. But the political balance having turned against them, they had to yield their place on the streets and wait until the promises of rehabilitation materialized.

Not every population group is able to operate successfully in political society and, as we have just seen, even when it is, its successes are often temporary. To give you an example of an organized group that clearly failed to make any headway in political society, let us move further north to the older part of the city—to College Street, where the old campus of the university is still located and which is the seat of the Bengali publishing industry. There is an entire neighborhood here of labyrinthine lanes and alleys where the principal activity is the printing, production, and selling of books. One can find an amazing mix of business organizations and technologies here, from large corporate houses with modern phototypesetting equipment to tiny owner-operated letterpresses where texts are still typeset by hand and where one could come upon a hand-operated treadle machine in perfect working order bearing the inscription "Made in Manchester 1882." In the 1990s, the letterpress was virtually wiped off the face of Calcutta—the effect of the global spread of electronic printing in every conceivable language and font. But another part of the publishing industry—bookbinding—continues to use technology that, in more than 120 years, has not changed in the slightest. We could walk into any of the binderies here and, except for the dim electric lamps and perhaps a transistor radio blaring film music, we could be in a nineteenth-century bookbinding workshop. An entire municipal ward here is called Daftaripara—the bookbinders' quarter—where there are 500 binderies employing 4,000 workers. My colleagues at the Centre for Studies in Social Sciences surveyed the bookbinders in 1990.[4]

There are many different kinds of bookbinding units and workers, coexisting for the most part on the bare margins of viability and frequently in competition with one another. The few large units have twenty or more workers each and floor space of 3,000 square feet or more. Their permanent workers are on monthly salaries that, in 1990, could go up to Rs.600 ($18) and enjoy the benefits of paid leave and pension. The vast majority of units are, however, of medium or small size, where the owners are also workers and there are often no more than two or three employees. Nearly a third of the workers are employed only during the peak business seasons. The average wages of skilled male workers in 1990 was around Rs.500 ($15) a month and that of the relatively unskilled women workers around Rs.400 ($12) if they worked a full eight hours a day. There are children too, employed as "boys" (regardless of gender, they are all "boys" here)—helping hands who could be engaged in all sorts of jobs from fetching tea to loading and unloading piles of books. They could earn about Rs.150 ($4.50) a month if they are paid in cash at all, because frequently all they get is food, clothes, and a place to sleep. These earnings are extremely low by the standards of industrial employment in India, but this is an unorganized industry lodged deep inside what is called the informal sector.

There were concerted attempts in the 1970s and 1980s to unionize the bookbinding workers and bargain with the owners for better pay. Activists of the Communist Party (Marxist) took a lead in this, especially after their party formed the state government in 1977. In 1990, there was a three-day strike in the binderies of Daftaripara. The form of the strike and its results are instructive. The workers demanded a wage increase of Rs.100 a month. But 90 percent of binderies were units whose owners were themselves workers. Everyone knew that most owners would never be able to pay the increased wage. The strike then became one in which the entire industry at Daftaripara—owners and workers together—tried to put pressure on publishers to pay more for binding jobs. The bigger publishers threatened to get their jobs done from other units in the city or even from outside the state. In the end, when the large binderies in Daftaripara agreed to increase wages by Rs.75 a month, the strikers declared a great victory and called off the agitation. Following the strike, union activities in Daftaripara were once more at a low ebb.

Unlike what we saw in the rail colony, there is very little sense in Daftaripara of a collective identity of bookbinders. Here are 4,000 people in the same trade, in a small urban neighborhood. Most of the men sleep in their workshops at night and go home to their villages on weekends and holidays. The women come from the suburbs, usually from refugee or squatter colonies like the one we saw earlier. They travel by train but cannot afford to buy tickets, choosing instead to flee when the conductors make an appearance. The workers in Daftaripara generally vote for the Left parties, but they know about politics from their rural connections, not because their lives as workers lead them to politics. Instead, they speak of ties of loyalty between owner and worker, of mutual acts of kindness, of paternal care. A retired worker, the venerable Habib Mia, speaks of the *inqilab* or revolution that had overtaken the country after the British left, so that now not even the wealthy and the propertied can take care of the poor.[5] But there is no engagement here with the apparatus of governmentality. The bookbinders of Daftaripara have not made their way into political society. Their example shows once more the difficulties of class organization in the so-called informal sector of labor, where the capitalist and the petty mode of production are intertwined in a mutually reinforcing tangle. Despite the sincere efforts of many activists, Leninist strategies of working-class organization have foundered here. The political leaders of the Left have instead turned their attention elsewhere and found much greater success—in political society.

II

The real story of political society must come from rural West Bengal. That is where the Left parties have converted the functions of governmentality into potent and amazingly stable sources of local support from a clear majority of population groups. Much has been written on how this was done—from land reforms to the institution of democratic local government in the villages to the maintenance of a tightly disciplined party organization to, as some critics allege, selective and carefully calibrated violence. But, for my discussion here, I will focus on the problem I raised in an earlier chapter: how can the particular claims of marginal population groups, often grounded in violations of the law, be made consistent with the pursuit of equal citizenship and civic virtue? To produce a viable and persuasive politics of the governed, there has to be a considerable act of mediation. Who can mediate?

You will remember the key figure in the successful mobilization of our rail colony into the arena of political society. He is the Master—the theatre enthusiast Anadi Bera. The fact that he was popularly known by his role as the teacher of a primary school is not insignificant. The school teacher was probably the most ubiquitous figure in the recent expansion of political society in rural West Bengal. In 1997, Dwaipayan Bhattacharya, one of my colleagues in Calcutta, studied the political role of school teachers in two districts of West Bengal.[6] In Purulia district, he found, most primary school teachers were members of the Communist teachers' association and many held elected positions at different levels of local government. They also held top posts in the party and the peasant organization and had been elected to the state legislature and parliament. Many of them were earlier associated with Gandhian organizations of social work. From the early 1980s, when the Communists pushed their land reforms and agricultural development programs, they wooed the school teachers, who soon were at the forefront of political activities in the district. With the traditional landlord class removed from the political scene, the teachers became crucial to the new politics of consensus that the Left was trying to build in rural West Bengal.

In the 1980s, a popular perception emerged everywhere that school teachers had the will and the ability to find commonly acceptable solutions to local disputes. Since they were salaried, they did not depend on agricultural incomes and thus did not have strong vested interests in land. Most came from peasant backgrounds and were thus thought to be sympathetic to the poor. They were the educated among a society of vast illiteracy. They were familiar with the language of peasants as well as that of the party, well versed in legal and administrative procedures, and yet organically part of the village community. As party leaders in local government, they were crucial in the implementation of governmental policies in the countryside. They interceded with the bureaucracy, using the language of administration, but claiming to speak on behalf of the poor. Simultaneously, they explained government policy and administrative decisions to the people of the village. Their views were frequently taken by government authorities to represent the local consensus: they recommended specific local forms of implementation of government programs, authenticated lists of local beneficiaries, and could be trusted to carry local opinion with them. In the 1980s, school teachers wielded unrivaled power and prestige in the rural districts. It was common to hear villagers saying that their school teacher was the one who most commanded their trust.

Now, before the admirers of Robert Putnam claim support in this evidence for the theory of social capital,[7] let me emphasize once more the distinction I am drawing between civic community in the sense of a liberal civil society and political society as I have described it. The rural poor who mobilize to claim the benefits of various governmental programs do not do so as members of civil society. To effectively direct those benefits toward them, they must succeed in applying the right pressure at the right places in the governmental machinery. This would frequently mean the bending or stretching of rules, because existing procedures have historically worked to exclude or marginalize them. They must, therefore, succeed in mobilizing population groups to produce a local political consensus that can effectively work *against* the distribution of power in society as a whole. This possibility is opened up by the working of political society. When school teachers gain the trust of the rural community to plead the case of the poor and secure the confidence of the administrators to find a local consensus that will stick, they do not embody the trust generated among equal members of a civic community. On the contrary, they mediate between domains that are differentiated by deep and historically entrenched inequalities of power. They mediate between those who govern and those who are governed.

I should add that when there is a successful mobilization of political society to secure the benefits of governmental programs for poor and underprivileged population groups, one could claim that there is an actual expansion of the freedoms of people, enabled by political society, that would not have been ordinarily possible within civil society. Ordinarily, governmental activity takes place within the stratified social structures of class, status, and privilege. Benefits that are meant to be available in general are effectively cornered by those who have greater knowledge of and influence over the system. This is so not only because of what may be described as corruption, that is, the criminal misuse of legal or administrative powers. Rather, it happens well within the normal ambit of legality because some sections of the people simply do not have the knowledge or the will to make claims to what they are entitled. This is a common state of affairs not only in countries like India where the effective civil society is limited to a small section of "proper" citizens. It is a well known experience in the operation of, let us say, the public health or education services in Western social democracies where the culturally equipped middle class is much better able to use the system than the poor or underprivileged. When the poor in countries like India, mobilized in political society, can affect the implementation of governmental activities in their favor, we must say that they have expanded their freedoms by using means that are not available to them in civil society.[8]

However, my story about school teachers is not a simple story with a happy ending—no story about political society ever is. Bhattacharya's study also found strong evidence of school teachers in rural West Bengal gradually losing the trust they once enjoyed. The state government allowed large pay increases to primary school teachers, all in the cause of improving primary education. If husband and wife were both primary school teachers, which was not uncommon, their combined cash income could be as large as that of the wealthiest village trader. By the early 1990s, the complaint was widespread that school teachers spent all their time in political work and did not teach. The teacher's job had become a lucrative one in rural society and there were allegations of kickbacks for teaching appointments. Once the trusted mediator, school teachers had now developed their own entrenched interests within the power structure. By the end of the 1990s, the Communist Party was clearly finding its teacher comrades a serious liability. The big question now is: how can political society renew itself? Who next will do the mediating?

III

The proper administration of governmental services has been a subject of much recent discussion in the fields of welfare and development. I will not consider here the neoliberal criticisms of the welfare state in Western democracies that have, in many cases, led to a significant reorganization of the sphere of governmentality. Rather, I will turn our attention to some new global technologies of governmentality that claim to ensure that the benefits of development are spread more evenly and that the poor and the underprivileged do not become its victims. This is an area where international development agencies in particular have recently reformulated their policies and refashioned their instruments in the light of their experience of the resistance to and the failures of various projects. I will focus, in particular, on the question of the resettlement and rehabilitation of populations displaced by development projects.

The World Bank has in the last two decades taken a leading role in formulating a rehabilitation policy and incorporating displacement and rehabilitation issues into project designs. Not surprisingly, following the basic logic of governmentality, the analysis of displacement costs and rehabilitation requirements was done mainly by the economic methods of cost-benefit analysis. At the same time, a set of entitlements was defined for project-affected persons or households losing their habitation or livelihoods. In addition, certain community-based entitlements were also defined for groups losing resources held in common or adversely affected in the performance of their cultural practices (such as losing their places of worship or sacred groves etc.). These entitlements were expected to be enforced through the government or the project-implementing agencies. In recent years, a new literature has emerged that seeks to expand the narrowly economic focus of the analysis of involuntary resettlement.[9] It includes elements such as landlessness, joblessness, homelessness, marginalization, food insecurity, increased morbidity and mortality, loss of access to common property, and social disarticulation, as possible consequences of displacement.

Theoretically, this recent reformulation owes a great deal to the capability approach to policy evaluation, embodying a set of substantive freedoms rather than utilities or incomes or primary goods, advocated by the economist Amartya Sen.[10] But devising objective measures of capabilities and practical operational procedures for targeting beneficiaries is not easy. There is also the problem of recognizing the claims of those who, like our rail colony squatters or street vendors, have no legal right to the space they have occupied. An interesting conceptual move that has tried to reorder the numerous ad hoc and paralegal solutions in this area is the distinction between *rights* and *entitlements*. Rights belong to those who have proper legal title to the lands or buildings that the authorities acquire; they are, we might say, proper citizens who must be paid the legally stipulated compensation. Those who do not have such rights may nevertheless have entitlements; they deserve not compensation but assistance in rebuilding a home or finding a new livelihood. The problem remains, however, of how these different kinds of rights and entitlements are to be identified and validated and how to ensure that the compensation or assistance reaches the right people.[11]

Faced with resistance by project-affected peoples and the failings of administratively dictated resettlement strategies, one persistent slogan has been to try to ensure the "participation" of the affected people in the rehabilitation process. Arguments have been made that, if carried out effectively and sincerely, this could turn involuntary resettlement into a voluntary one. It has also been argued that although resettlement costs as included within project costs are higher in voluntary resettlements, the projects tend to be more efficient and successful in the end because they can be completed on time and the social and political problems of incomplete rehabilitation can be avoided. The point has now become so much of a cliché in the literature that it is repeated almost as a mantra—by government agencies, funding institutions, project consultants, experts, and activists. Most statements on this point end up by merely repeating the new liberal dogma: "participation of civil society through NGOs." Participation, however, has one meaning when it is seen from the standpoint of those who govern, i.e., as a category of governance. It will have a very different meaning when seen from the position of the governed, i.e., as a practice of democracy.

To give you a sense of some of the conditions of possibility of democracy as the politics of the governed, let me bring you three cases of resettlement that I studied in 2000.[12]

The first case is from the coal mine town of Raniganj near the western border of Bengal with Bihar. The air hangs heavy here with smoke and at night you can see the fires burning in the distant fields. Large settled areas, including densely populated urban areas, are prone to subsidence and underground and surface fires because of decades of indiscriminate mining. Following several minor and not so minor disasters, efforts have been under way to stabilize the surface and prevent the fires. However, the methods are technically difficult, slow, and extremely expensive. The alternative is to resettle the population at safer locations. After prolonged discussion and some local agitation, the government of India appointed in 1996 a high-level committee, which reported that more than 34,000 houses in 151 locations were in critically unstable areas. The cost of resettlement for about 300,000 people, including housing, land, infrastructure, and shifting allowance, and with no compensation for those who had no legal title, would be about Rs.20 billion ($500 million). It advised that in view of the "urgency" of the matter, resettlement should begin immediately without waiting for the institutional machinery to be put in place.

Apparently, the resettlement work is in progress, but no one in the area could show me any visible signs and most didn't even seem to know. There is a vague sense of the possibility of large-scale disaster, but the people here have lived with this danger for decades and don't seem to be greatly concerned. Resettlement is not tied here with a new developmental project or with new economic opportunities. If there is a sense in the government and public sector agencies that resettlement needs to be carried out as a means of preventing a sudden and massive disaster, there is little urgency in this regard within the population. There does not seem to be any evidence of a "voluntary" move for resettlement. Political society has not been mobilized here to benefit the people.

My second case is from the port and new industrial town of Haldia, across the river from, and to the south of, Calcutta. The Haldia resettlement took place in two phases for two very different projects. The contrast between the two experiences is instructive.

First, land was acquired for the construction of Haldia port from 1963 to 1984. The process of acquisition and resettlement was long, slow, and marked by numerous difficulties including many disputes that ended up in court. Earlier, not everyone who qualified was interested in taking the resettlement plots since they were not conveniently located in relation to their places of agricultural work. In the early 1990s, with the rapid rise in land prices following the urbanization of the Haldia area, there was a rush of applications for the resettlement plots, some from people (or their sons and daughters) who had been dislocated twenty-five before. As of 2000, more than 1,400 of the original 2,600 families who qualified still remained to be resettled, more than twenty years after their lands were taken.

The next phase of land acquisition came with the new industrialization of Haldia in 1988–91, leading to considerable organized agitation demanding resettlement. In 1995, it was decided that rehabilitation cases would be dealt with on the recommendations of a Rehabilitation Advisory Committee. The Committee would consist of two administrators, two land acquisition officers, and four political persons representing the main government and opposition parties. All processing of applications for resettlement, hearing of cases, allotments, dealing with grievances, were to be done by this committee.

The general impression among administrators, political leaders and affected persons seems to be that this has been a successful procedure. The idea is that the task of formulating the specific norms, under prevailing local circumstances, of qualifying for rehabilitation plots and of identifying genuine cases deserving rehabilitation should be done on the basis of a ground-level agreement between political representatives. Since the agreement would involve both the government party and the party of opposition, it could be assumed that this would represent an effective local consensus. Once an agreement was reached at this level, the task of the administration was simply to carry out the decisions.

The important assumption here is, of course, that the political parties effectively cover the entire range of interests and opinions. Given the highly politicized, organized, and polarized nature of rural society in most of West Bengal today, this may not be an unwarranted assumption. If there was a third organized political force in the area which also represented a distinct set of voices, it would also have had to be accommodated within such a committee if it was to be effective.

The Committee decided, for instance, that the minimum rehabilitation plot would be 0.04 acres, that families with a larger number of dependents would get larger plots, that no one could get cash instead of rehabilitation plots, that those who owned houses elsewhere would not qualify, that those who had built structures on their homesteads in anticipation of the land being acquired would not qualify, etc. All of these matters were decided on the basis of local investigations and the feeling was that if both political parties were represented, there was no way that the qualification criteria could be misapplied. The Committee also decided that particular plots in the rehabilitation areas would be drawn by lottery, with the displaced persons drawing their own lots. Consequently, there could be no complaints that particular individuals had been favored with better located plots. Looking through the decisions made by the committee, I even found cases where it reversed its earlier decisions in the light of new information brought to its notice by the political representatives and one case where a woman was given a rehabilitation plot on humanitarian grounds even though she did not meet the stipulated norms.

My third resettlement case is from Rajarhat, to the northeast of Calcutta, where a new town is coming up. In the course of only a few years, it is being transformed from a rural agricultural area to a virtual extension of the Calcutta urban metropolis. As a result, land prices in the area have skyrocketed. As soon as news spread of the New Town project, property developers and land speculators swooped on the small landowners and tried to buy them out before the land acquisition process began. Apart from the rapidly soaring land prices, another problem was that all values of land sales in urban and semi-urban areas are routinely under-recorded for registration purposes in order to avoid taxes. The official decision was to encourage voluntary resettlement by offering market prices. But if market prices were determined by the legal records of land sales in the area, no one would be induced to part with their lands voluntarily.

The decision was then made to acquire land at "negotiated" prices. A Land Procurement Committee was set up to negotiate an acceptable price with the affected persons. Not surprisingly, the Committee included local representatives of the government as well as the opposition political parties. The result, it is claimed, is a virtually trouble-free acquisition with almost no court cases. Owners were compensated within three months (since there was no official price fixing)—this was a record by any standards. The cost of acquisition was certainly higher than would have been the case if the normal legal procedure had been followed. But then the project would have been delayed. And since the object of the project was to develop new urban land for sale, the increased cost could be absorbed in the prices to be charged from those who would be given the developed lands.[13]

This is political society in an active relationship with the procedures of governmentality. Political society has here found a place in the general political culture. Here, people are not unaware of their possible entitlements or ignorant of the means of making themselves heard. Rather, they have formally recognized political representatives who they can use to mediate on their behalf. However, the form will work only if all have a stake in the success of the particular project, or else some mediators will wreck the consensus. Further, the form is likely to work only if the governmental authority follows the recommendations of the political representatives but is itself outside the ambit of electoral politics. That is to say, the governmental body and the political body must be kept separate but put in a relationship in which the latter can influence the former. But the distinction between the governmental and the political must be clearly maintained.

The decisions recorded by the governmental authorities hide the actual negotiations that must have taken place in political society. We are not told on what specific criteria the political representatives finally agreed on the list of beneficiaries. It is entirely possible that the negotiations on the ground did not respect the principles of bureaucratic rationality or even the provisions of the law. We know that in one case at least a person was included in the list of beneficiaries because the representatives felt she deserved to be on it even though she did not qualify according to the prescribed norms. In Rajarhat, we know from other sources that the local consensus includes an understanding that a part of the compensation to be paid to the owners of land would be distributed to tenants and laborers who have lost their livelihoods. This is entirely beyond the purview of what the governmental authority needs to recognize, or even know, but it presupposes it by accepting the recommendations of the political representatives.

We must also remember that a local consensus among rival political representatives is likely to reflect the locally dominant interests and values. It would be effective in securing the demands of those who are able to find organized political support, but could ignore and even suppress demands of locally marginalized interests. Besides, let us not forget that a local political consensus is also likely to be socially conservative and could be particularly insensitive, for instance, to gender or minority issues. As I have mentioned a few times before, political society will bring into the hallways and corridors of power some of the squalor, ugliness and violence of popular life. But if one truly values the freedom and equality that democracy promises, then one cannot imprison it within the sanitized fortress of civil society.

You may have noticed that when I describe political society as a site of negotiation and contestation opened up by the activities of governmental agencies aimed at population groups, I frequently talk of administrative processes that are *paralegal* and of collective claims that appeal to ties of *moral solidarity*. It is important, I think, to emphasize once more how political society is located in relation to the legal-political forms of the modern state itself. The ideals of popular sovereignty and equal citizenship enshrined within the modern state are, as I have mentioned in an earlier chapter, mediated by and realized through the two dimensions of property and community. Property is the conceptual name of the regulation by law of relations between individuals in civil society. Even where social relations are not, or have not yet been, molded into the proper forms of civil society, the state must nevertheless maintain the fiction that in the constitution of its sovereignty, all citizens belong to civil society and are, by virtue of that legally constructed fact, equal subjects of the law. Yet in the actual administration of governmental services, as we have repeatedly noticed, the fictive quality of this legal construct must be recognized and dealt with. What results is a dual strategy: on the one hand, paralegal arrangements that modify, rearrange or supplement on the contingent terrain of political society the formal structures of property that must, on the other hand, continue to be affirmed and protected within the legally constituted domain of civil society. Property is, we know, the crucial dimension along which capital overlaps with the modern state. It is over property then that we see, on the terrain of political society, a dynamic *within* the modern state of the transformation of precapitalist structures and of premodern cultures. It is there that we can observe a struggle over the real, rather than the merely formal, distribution of rights among citizens. Consequently, it is in political society that we are able to discern the shifting historical horizon of political modernity in most of the world, where just as the fictive ideal of civil society may wield a powerful influence on the forces of political change, so can the actual transactions over the everyday distribution of rights and entitlements lead over time to substantial redefinitions of property and law within the actually existing modern state. The paralegal then, despite its ambiguous and supplementary status in relation to the legal, is not some pathological condition of retarded modernity, but rather part of the very process of the historical constitution of modernity in most of the world.

Community, on the other hand, is conferred legitimacy within the domain of the modern state only in the form of the nation. Other solidarities that could potentially come into conflict with the political community of the nation are subject to a great deal of suspicion. We have seen, however, that the activities of governmental functions produce numerous classes of actual populations that come together to act politically. To effectively make its claim in political society, a population group produced by governmentality must be invested with the moral content of community. This is a major part of the politics of governmentality. Here there are many imaginative possibilities for transforming an empirically assembled population group into the morally constituted form of a community. I have already argued that it is both unrealistic and irresponsible to condemn all such political transformations as divisive and dangerous.

However, I have not told you very much at all about the dark side of political society. That is not because I am unaware of its existence but because I cannot claim to fully understand how criminality or violence are tied to the ways in which various deprived population groups must struggle to make their claims to governmental care. I believe I have said enough about political society to suggest that in the field of popular democratic practice, crime and violence are not fixed black-and-white legal categories; they could be open to a great deal of political negotiation. It is a fact, for instance, that in the last two and a half decades, there has been a distinct rise in the public, and political, outbreak of caste violence in India, in a period which has seen without doubt the most rapid expansion of democratic assertion by the hitherto oppressed castes. We also have numerous examples when violent movements by deprived regional, tribal or other minority groups have been followed by a quick and often generous inclusion into the ambit of governmentality. Is there then a strategic use of illegality and violence here, on the terrain of political society, that has led one internationally acclaimed writer to describe Indian democracy, not very sympathetically, as "a million mutinies now"? I don't have a good answer. However, an insightful recent study of this question has been published by Thomas Blom Hansen on the Shiv Sena in Mumbai. Aditya Nigam has also published some recent papers dealing with the "underground" of civil society. For the moment, I can only refer you to these works.[14]

I have used examples from only one small region of India. That is because it is the region I know best. It is also a region where, I think, political society has taken a distinct form within the evolving popular culture of democratic politics. In the light of that experience, I have tried to think about some of the conditions in which the functions of governmentality can create conditions not for a contraction but rather an expansion of democratic political participation. It is not insignificant that India is the only major democracy in the world where electoral participation has continued to increase in recent years and is actually increasing faster among the poor, the minorities, and the disadvantaged population groups. There is also some recent evidence of a fall in participation among the rich and the urban middle classes.[15] This suggests a very different political response to the facts of governmentality than in most Western democracies.

I have also not said anything here about gender. Fortunately, this is a subject on which there is a flourishing and sophisticated literature in the context of Indian democracy.[16] Interestingly, it is often the darker side of political society that is at issue here. There was, for instance, a spate of progressive legislation in the 1980s, advocated by women's groups and quickly adopted by parliament, to ensure greater rights for women. The question has now been raised if this was not a success won too easily, by legislative action from the top, because the actual lives of most women are still led in families and communities where everyday practices are regulated not by the law but by other authorities. The question has been raised if the rights of women in minority communities are best furthered by state legislation that might even violate minority rights, or whether the only viable road is the slow and painstaking one of trying to change beliefs and practices within the minority communities themselves. A proposal to reserve a third of the seats in parliament for women has been recently stalled by the vociferous opposition of backward caste leaders who have alleged that it would whittle away their hard-earned representation and substitute it by upper-caste women legislators. In this, as in many other issues concerning women's rights, one can discern the inescapable conflict between the enlightened desires of civil society and the messy, contentious, and often unpalatable concerns of political society.

I conclude by reminding my readers of the founding moment of the political theory of democracy in ancient Greece. Centuries before either civil society or liberalism was invented, Aristotle had concluded that not all persons were fit to become part of the governing class because not everyone had the necessary practical wisdom or ethical virtue. But his shrewd empirical mind did not rule out the possibility that in some societies, for some kinds of people, under some conditions, democracy might be a good form of government. Our political theory today does not accept Aristotle's criteria of the ideal constitution. But our actual governmental practices are still based on the premise that not everyone can govern. What I have tried to show is that alongside the abstract promise of popular sovereignty, people in most of the world are devising new ways in which they can choose how they should be governed. Many of the forms of political society I have described would not, I suspect, meet with Aristotle's approval, because they would appear to him to allow popular leaders to take precedence over the law. But we might, I think, be able to persuade him that in this way the people are learning, and forcing their governors to learn, how they would prefer to be governed. That, the wise Greek might agree, is a good ethical justification for democracy.

London-style double-decker bus veers around a bullock cart. (Ahmed Ali, 1952) AHMED ALI; HITESRANJAN SANYAL MEMORIAL ARCHIVE OF THE CENTRE FOR STUDIES IN SOCIAL SCIENCES, CALCUTTA,

The modern work place: Coca-Cola advertisement. (Ahmed Ali, 1953) AHMED ALI; HITESRANJAN SANYAL MEMORIAL ARCHIVE OF THE CENTRE FOR STUDIES IN SOCIAL SCIENCES, CALCUTTA

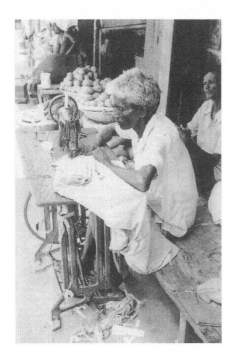

A pavement tailor. (Subrata Lahiri, 1977) CHITRABANI; HITESRANJAN SANYAL MEMORIAL ARCHIVE OF THE CENTRE FOR STUDIES IN SOCIAL SCIENCES, CALCUTTA

A fruit market on the street. (Subrata Lahiri, 1977) Chitrabani; Hitesranjan Sanyal Memorial Archive of the Centre for Studies in Social Sciences, Calcutta

Pavement typists. (Salim Paul, 1977) CHITRABANI; HITESRANJAN SANYAL MEMORIAL ARCHIVE
OF THE CENTRE FOR STUDIES IN SOCIAL SCIENCES, CALCUTTA

Food stalls. (Subrata Lahiri, 1977) CHITRABANI; HITESRANJAN SANYAL MEMORIAL ARCHIVE OF
THE CENTRE FOR STUDIES IN SOCIAL SCIENCES, CALCUTTA

Selling juice. (Subrata Lahiri, 1977)   Chitrabani; Hitesranjan Sanyal Memorial Archive
of the Centre for Studies in Social Sciences, Calcutta

Selling lottery tickets. Business is not brisk. (Amit Dhar, 1977)   Chitrabani; Hitesranjan
Sanyal Memorial Archive of the Centre for Studies in Social Sciences, Calcutta

A squatter settlement on railway land. (Sabuj Mukhopadhyay, 2003)
SABUJ MUKHOPADHYAY

Domestic life goes on inches away from the railway tracks. (Sabuj Mukhopadhyay, 2003)
SABUJ MUKHOPADHYAY

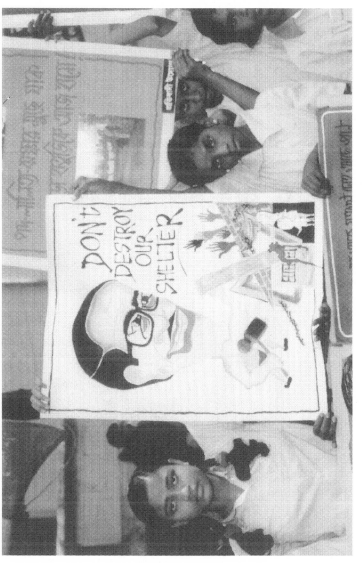

Children from squatter colonies demonstrate to save their homes. (Sabuj Mukhopadhyay, 2002)

SABUJ MUKHOPADHYAY

A bookbinding workshop. (Bikash Bose, 2003)

A printing press. Little has changed in a hundred years. (Bikash Bose, 2003)

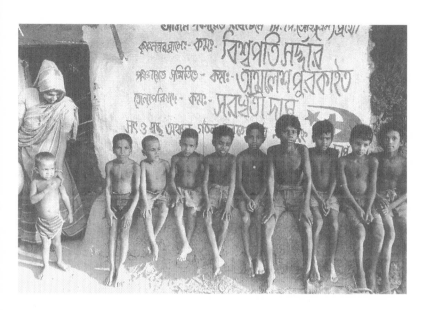

Slogans on the wall for village council elections. (Dilip Banerjee, 1993)   DILIP BANERJEE

The hammer and sickle in rural Bengal. (Dilip Banerjee, 1993)   DILIP BANERJEE

Advertising the new metropolitan lifestyle. (2003)

Graffiti showing shackled Indian minister, bent under the burden of IMF loans. (Amit Dhar, 1984)
Chitrabani; Hitesranjan Sanyal Memorial Archive of the Centre for Studies in Social Sciences, Calcutta

PART II

GLOBAL/LOCAL:
Before and After September 11

FOUR

The World After the Great Peace

I

When I entered Presidency College, Calcutta, in 1964, Professor
Susobhan Sarkar had left for Jadavpur University. But he was by then
a legend among students of the college. It is my misfortune that as a
student and researcher I only saw him a few times from a distance
and never had the chance to know him well. But I noticed among my
elder historian colleagues the unmistakable imprint of his influence.
Although his best known published writings are his essays on the
Bengal renaissance,[1] he was really a teacher of European history. Year
after year, it was his lectures on European history and politics that
created his enormous reputation among students. In the *festschrift* to
Susobhan Sarkar, Professor Barun De remarked that Bengali intellectuals of the 1930s and 1940s were less interested in Bengal's agrarian
economy or peasant movements than in world politics or European
philosophy and literature. Their minds were then far more open to
the outside world.[2] These days, we are told, things are quite the opposite. Bengali intellectuals today allegedly prefer to live as frogs inside
their own well. I am not sure if the complaint is justified, but nevertheless I shall follow the example of Susobhan Sarkar and take up
here the subject of world history.

The Susobhan Sarkar Memorial Lecture 2001, organized by the Paschim Banga
Itihas Samsad and delivered on August 18, 2001, at Presidency College, Calcutta.
Translated from the Bengali by the author.

The title of this chapter echoes the title of Professor Sarkar's first published book, written in Bengali, entitled *Europe After the Great War* (1939).[3] The book is now hard to find. I had a chance to look at it some thirty years ago, and I still remember it well. In it, Sarkar analyzed European politics from the end of World War I to 1938. From today's perspective it could easily have been titled *Europe Before the Second Great War*. Sarkar's analysis contained a clear premonition of the impending conflict.

I will begin by taking stock of where human history has arrived at the turn of the millennium. There are two conflicting assessments in circulation at present. The first goes as follows. Modernity and its forms of life, based on industrialization, the advance of science, and the free flowering of the individual spirit, should by now have spread all over the globe. The reason why it has not is that certain regimes and ideologies, overly committed to state control, had entrenched themselves in different countries of the world. This had led in the twentieth century to two world wars and a terrible cold war. (Sometimes the cold war got a little hot, as in Vietnam.) Millions of people were denied the benefits and pleasures of modernity. Finally, in the last decade of the millennium, those backward-looking regimes collapsed under the weight of their own inefficiencies. The dark days of the cold war came to an end. The whole world rejoiced in the invigorating light of the free market and liberal politics. Human history entered the era of the Great Peace.

The second assessment, needless to say, does not paint quite as joyful a picture. This story runs as follows. Various forms of socialism had been tried out in different countries of the Second and Third Worlds in the belief that independent socioeconomic progress, outside the command of monopoly capital and imperialism, was possible. Not all of those trials were successful. The main impediment to their success was the incessant opposition put up by monopoly capital and imperialism. Under the cover of the cold war, capital expanded, conquered new markets, and satisfied its lust for greater profits. In the end, lust won out. The struggle against an all-consuming capitalism and the dream of emancipation lived on only as a memory. A dark shadow—the Great Peace—descended on earth.

These are two contradictory story lines. But there is little dispute about naming the event that they describe. Whatever one's normative judgment on it, everyone seems to agree that what is happening all over the world in the last few years is best called globalization. I am told that the word "globalization" was first used in the mid-1970s by American Express—in an advertisement for their credit cards. Some of us believed in our callow youth that the decade of the 1970s would be the decade of liberation. It now appears that even American banks had the same dream. For the time being at least, the bankers' dream has turned out to be true. If you have an American Express credit card in your pocket, you would feel sufficiently liberated to shop to your heart's content in any country of the world.

But to say that this is globalization is to fail to understand its process. More crucially, the mere name does not tell us what we should do when we are faced with it. Are we to surrender to it? Embrace it with both arms? Or are we to turn away from it? Or perhaps even roll up our sleeves and prepare to punch it in the face? Needless to say, the answer depends on how we understand and evaluate the process called globalization. The two assessments I mentioned a little while ago are assessments from two diametrically opposed positions. The actual situation is without doubt somewhere in the middle. But where exactly is it located? Many thinkers are grappling with this matter today. I will try and give you my understanding of what they have been saying. It is not as though only laissez-faire liberals have written on the subject. Many leftist and Marxist writers have also looked closely and seriously at the phenomenon called globalization—for instance, geographers such as Manuel Castels and David Harvey, or sociologists such as Saskia Sassen and David Held, or even literary theorists such as Frederick Jameson and Gayatri Chakravorty Spivak. It is useless here to look for reliable knowledge confirmed beyond doubt. Rather, those who claim to possess confirmed theories on this subject are most probably driven by dubious motives.

II

Let us begin with a historical question. What is new about globalization? If the process means that different geographical regions of the world have become dependent on one another—that they have be-

come entangled in a huge net of circulation of commodities and services—then that is a process that has gone on for at least 200 years.
Many years ago, Karl Marx and Frederick Engels wrote in *The Communist Manifesto* that the owners of capital would stalk the world in
search of new markets. "It must nestle everywhere, settle everywhere,
establish connections everywhere." Old and established national industries will be destroyed. Production and consumption in every
country will become cosmopolitan and global. "To the great chagrin
of reactionaries, [the bourgeoisie] has drawn from under the feet of
industry the national ground on which it stood." The new industries
will no longer use indigenous raw material; their raw material will
come from the remotest corners of the earth. Similarly, their products
will be consumed not only at home but in all quarters of the globe
as well.[4] This was in 1848. One might say that globalization was already
quite advanced then. So what is new today?

There is an ongoing debate over this question.[5] The evidence of
history shows that there indeed was a major globalization at the end
of the nineteenth century. Large amounts of capital were being ex-
ported from Europe to many parts of the world, especially to North
and South America and to the British and French colonies. It was the
increasing international flow of capital that pushed most large countries to accept from the 1870s a common gold standard for fixing the
exchange rate of their currencies. Many scholars have argued that the
rate of export of capital at the end of the twentieth century was actually lower than that at the end of the nineteenth. If one takes the
fifteen most developed countries, it turns out that in the 1880s, foreign
capital accounted for as much as 5 percent of their total national
incomes. In the 1930s, this figure had come down to 1.5 percent, and
in the 1950s and 1960s to 1 percent. In 1996, when the triumphal
drumbeats of globalization were splitting our ears, the proportion of
foreign capital to the combined national incomes of those fifteen
developed countries had not even climbed back to 2.5 percent, that
is to say, to half the level of the 1880s. If one takes just the case of
Britain, we find that between 1895 to 1899, as much as 21 percent of
British savings was invested abroad. Between 1910 and 1913, the figure
had gone up to 53 percent. At the time, as much as one-fourth of all

British capital was invested abroad. No developed industrial country is as dependent today on international capital transactions. Even Argentina, which at the end of the nineteenth century had half of its capital owned by foreigners, now has only 20 to 22 percent foreign capital employed in its economy, even though we hear everyday that it is sinking under the burden of its international debts.

In other words, if we consider the flow of international capital, there is actually less globalization today than there was at the end of the nineteenth century. Needless to say, the export of capital and the international financial markets were greatly disrupted after World War I. This was followed by the worldwide depression of the 1930s. The gold standard, for all practical purposes, became inoperative. It was the Bretton Woods arrangement after World War II that attempted to restore some order and control to international financial exchanges. There was, therefore, an ebb in globalization until the 1970s. The tide began to rise again only in the 1980s. The celebrations over globalization today are thus largely a result of comparisons made with the situation in the middle decades of the twentieth century, not with that in the nineteenth.

Moving from the export of capital to international trade, we see more or less the same kind of picture. International trade expanded through all of the nineteenth century until World War I and then contracted in the middle of the twentieth century. It began to grow again from around 1975. Britain, France, Japan, Germany, the United States, Canada—all of these countries were engaged in international trade at much higher levels before World War I than they were in 1970. Since the 1980s, of course, they have all reached those levels and, in some cases, even surpassed them.

All of this relates, needless to say, to the industrialized countries of Europe and America. The picture is less clear for other countries. Most countries in Asia have become deeply entangled with the global economy in the last ten or fifteen years. On the other hand, nearly half of the countries of Africa seem to have lost their connections with international trade. Thus, one thing is clear: globalization is not some great carnival of capital, technology, and goods where we are all free to walk away with what we want. What one gets and how much, where one finds a place in the global network of exchanges, indeed whether one finds a place in it at all, depends on several economic and political conditions.

The promoters of globalization insist, of course, that by linking up with the global economy, poorer countries can get richer and the inequalities between countries can be brought down. Has that happened? The evidence is not conclusive. If one set of researchers produce one set of figures to say that inequalities between countries have actually increased because of globalization, then another set of researchers will immediately counter this with another set of figures to argue that inequalities have not increased and in fact will soon go down. For us ignorant people, there is little to do but stare blankly at the two sets of figures. My own impression from all that I have heard and seen is that, on balance, inequalities between rich and poor countries have not come down in the last ten or fifteen years; if anything, they have probably increased. Not only that, some countries that were developing rapidly a few years ago have recently tripped at the hurdles and slowed down considerably. In the 1970s, several countries in South America had advanced at great pace precisely by engaging in foreign trade. They were laid low in the 1980s by the burden of foreign debts; most have not recovered since. The economic advance of East Asia in the 1980s became legendary. And then suddenly in 1997, disaster struck those economies. The crisis has not been fully averted. Why there are these sudden reversals of fortune and whether they are inevitable in the period of globalization are questions we must address later.

In addition to financial and trade networks, there are two other aspects of globalization that one hears about a great deal: these are communications and travel. Both are crucial in evaluating the cultural consequences of globalization. There is little doubt that the movement of people across national boundaries has greatly increased because of improvements in transportation. International travel is no longer restricted to merchants and maharajas. Millions of ordinary people now go out on international voyages. However, if we look specifically at international migration (rather than mere travel), it turns out that there were more people who migrated to and settled down in other countries in the nineteenth century than did so at the end of the twentieth. In the years from 1820 to World War I, sixty million people migrated from Europe to the Americas. Needless to say, the bulk of the present inhabitants of the United States, Canada, Argentina, Australia, or New Zealand are descendants of these nineteenth-century migrants. In addition, there were some twenty to thirty million Indians who were taken to Malaya, Fiji, Mauritius, different countries of Africa, and to the West Indies as indentured laborers. The evidence shows that in the first decade of the twentieth century, a million people migrated each year from one country to another. After World War II, there was a new demand for immigrant laborers in low-wage work in the industrial countries of the West. As a result, the flow of foreign immigrants into these countries continues today through both legal and illegal channels. But if one considers the numbers, the level of international migration today is actually lower than that before World War I.

The historical evidence shows, therefore, that in several aspects and at least in quantitative terms, globalization was actually more advanced in the period before World War I than it is now. It is well known, of course, that the period leading up to that War constitutes an important chapter in the story of the evolution of global capital. We know, especially from Lenin's writings, that the period was characterized by the great influence of finance capital and the rivalries between the imperialist powers. Could it be that the wheel of world history is turning us back to that earlier phase? Or is it the case that there has been in the meantime such a transformation in the nature of capital and the state that despite the apparent similarities, the two periods of globalization are quite different in character? Let us, then, look at the differences.

To understand the character of capital at the beginning of the twenty-first century, we must look not so much at industrial capital but at the international financial markets. A major pressure exerted by the forces of globalization today is to loosen the controls of the national state over the financial and banking system of the country, to free the circuits of international capital in and out of the country, and to improve the computer and telecommunications infrastructure.

This has resulted in an incredibly rapid expansion of the international capital markets bringing about a revolution in the development of capital. Since 1980, finance capital in the rich industrialized countries of the world has grown at a rate that is two-and-a-half times that of the national product. The trade in currencies, bonds, and equities has increased at five times the rate of increase in the national product. In other words, more and more capital is being invested in the trade of stocks, bonds, and currencies than in manufacturing, presumably because the profits are quicker and greater. In fact, the biggest financial market today is the currency market, which is truly global in its scope and operation. In 1983, the trade in currencies was ten times larger in volume than the total volume of international trade in commodities; in 1992, it was sixty times larger. Then there is the international trade in bonds. In the early 1980s, the annual trade in U.S. treasury bonds was around $30 billion; in the early 1990s, this had gone up to $500 billion. The buying of U.S. treasury bonds has continued to rise, and along with it the U.S. foreign debt. But that is not a cause of much worry for the leaders of that country. The advantage of being the only superpower in the world is that its foreign debt is not necessarily a burden but one more instrument of wielding power.

Is there a limit to this amazingly rapid expansion of the international financial market? Can the flow of capital across national boundaries grow indefinitely at this speed? Many experts think that the growth of the financial markets will continue for some time to come. In 1992, the global financial market was twice as large as the combined national product of the twenty-three richest countries of the world. In 2000, it was three times as large. The MacKinsey Global Institute predicts that the financial markets can continue growing at this rate for at least another twenty years, because many national markets are yet to be integrated within the global financial system.

Of course, there are many risks involved in speculating with bonds and currencies. One example is the case of the Baring Company, a venerable financial institution that was laid low by an ill-advised transaction made by an overenthusiastic and somewhat unscrupulous employee. While the stock market boom of the 1990s is over, that is hardly a reason for capital to shut up shop and stay at home. Capital today appears to be searching once more for that primordial world-conquering spirit that characterized its early years. But even if the spirit is primordial, its skills are much sharper and more sophisticated. Famous economists are now working day and night trying to devise scientific ways of managing risks in the financial markets. One or two of them have even won the Nobel Prize for their efforts. Who says capital has no regard for scholarship? It has great regard for scholarship that contributes to profits. Referring to the influence of finance capital before World War I, Keynes said that it was turning the national economies into gambling dens. Today, many economists are saying, "Keynes Sahib, fear not! We have now mastered the science of gambling. The markets will grow, our profits will grow, capital will flourish, we shall all be deliriously happy."

If we compare the global financial market today with that in the early twentieth century, three significant differences emerge. First, because of our present information and telecommunication technologies, currencies or stocks can be instantaneously bought and sold across countries. As a result, there is much greater opportunity today to take advantage of price fluctuations in stocks, bonds, and currencies in different markets around the world. The total volume of daily transactions is also many times larger today. The daily flow of international capital across national boundaries is considerably higher. Second, the markets in financial capital are dominated by a few major institutions such as insurance companies, pension funds, mutual funds, etc. These institutions pool together the small savings of ordinary people and invest them in profitable ventures. Third, many new instruments of financial transaction have been invented in the last two or three decades. Many things that could not have been imagined as items of exchange twenty years ago are now being traded for millions of dollars. For instance, derivatives. I have often asked my economist friends to explain to me the nature of this mysterious commodity. In spite of their best efforts, I must confess that the subject still eludes my old-fashioned college teacher's powers of comprehension.

Alongside these revolutionary changes in the global financial markets, the globalization of manufacturing has proceeded steadily in the last thirty years. The manufacture of different components of a prod-

uct in factories located in different countries and the assembling of
the final product in yet another country is now entirely common-
place. The globalization of manufacturing processes is particularly
advanced in the automobile, chemical, pharmaceutical, and electronics industries. Even something so traditional as the manufacture of
textiles is now dispersed across many countries. In Bangladesh, for
instance, the word *garment* has now become an everyday folksy Bengali word: it means a factory for manufacturing clothes for export.
But this kind of globalization of manufacturing, as I said, has been
happening for a few decades. What is new is the global dispersal of
services such as accounting and administration. Think of a company
that has its head office in London, but whose staff payrolls are com-
puted and administered in Bangalore, whose phone calls from cus-
tomers are answered in Singapore, and whose sales figures and in-
ventories are maintained in Buenos Aires. This is not science fiction.
Even someone as ignorant in business matters as me has read and
heard about many such companies. But the fact that the manufacturing and service components of a firm are dispersed in many parts
of the world does not mean that the company is being decentralized.
As a crucial aspect of this globalization process, there is actually a
huge centralization of control and profit earning. In fact, the more
the different parts of manufacturing and services are being spread
across different countries, the greater the need for centralized control.
What is significant is that the centralized control is invariably located
in the metropolitan cities of the industrialized world. One of the
strange consequences of globalization is the enormous importance of
a few cities like New York, London, Paris, or Tokyo—Saskia Sassen
has called them "global cities."[6] So we have, on the one hand, a dispersal across the world of component parts of the manufacturing and
service activities of firms and, on the other hand, a growing centralized control over all these activities from a few head offices located
in the global cities.

What then about the control of the national state over the national
economy? We have always known that modern national economies
are framed and regulated by laws made by the state. Are those days
over? Who will now make the laws to regulate the economy? Perhaps

this is the most important question that faces us today in relation to the political aspects of globalization.

III

It is commonly agreed today that the global economy is exerting a deep and aggressive influence on the internal policies of all nation-states. The greatest influence is exerted by the institutions that control the international flow of finance. This form of capital can travel at great speed from one country to another. As a result, in the case of those countries that are particularly dependent on international capital, the global financial institutions can extract the policies they want by threatening to move their money out of those countries. Needless to say, countries that land in a financial crisis are often forced to accept the conditions imposed by international lending institutions in exchange for a rescue package. There is no doubt that the result is an undermining of national sovereignty. The question is: should a possible threat to national sovereignty persuade countries to stay away from the process of globalization? It appears, however, that the costs of staying away are also huge and few states have the resources to accept them. One might argue that a state could use the power of its laws to erect barriers around its national economy to protect it from the uncertainties of the global market and the dangerous influence of international finance capital. But the result inevitably is a series of unavoidable and mounting budget deficits, inflation, rise in the national debt, shortage of foreign currency, and in the end a major financial crisis. To escape from the crisis, the government has to approach the international financial institutions for loans. The doors and windows of the hitherto walled-up economy begin to open one after the other. Once the doors open, it becomes difficult to conceal the seductive appeal of globalization. The elite and the middle classes are the first to protest: "Why should our standards of living and the quality of our goods and services be so low?" they begin to ask. "Let us join the global markets, increase our ties with the outside world, import new technologies. Let us end the miserable dullness of our consumer life," they demand. In the last twenty years, almost no country in the world has been able to avoid this process. It led to the collapse of the socialist state in the Soviet Union and Eastern Europe. The economy of China is today deeply enmeshed in the network of globalization. Although the Communist Party still remains in power there, no one talks of socialism any more. Cuba largely remains outside the network, but this is less the result of its own choice and more because of the economic boycott and political opposition put up by the United States. North Korea still has its doors closed. One cannot say that the results are anything to cheer about.

In other words, globalization is something like the proverbial *laddus* of Delhi: those who eat them land in trouble; those who don't eat them also land in trouble.[7] That staying away altogether from the global economy leads to serious trouble seems to be verified truth. Whether it is possible to avoid trouble after entering the global economy depends on how greatly we value the sovereignty of the national state. Many now say that sovereignty is a thing of the past. What good is sovereignty if it does not enable us to feed and clothe our people well? Besides, it is also true that ruling groups in many countries use the pretext of national sovereignty to impose ruthless tyrannies on their people. In such cases, the argument that national sovereignty is inviolable becomes a tool in the hands of reactionaries. Can we therefore defend sovereignty universally without also considering the specific circumstances in which it is being applied? There are many important thinkers who have raised such questions recently. Let us give them a hearing before we decide to throw the arguments out of court.

The sovereign state was created in the modern sense in Europe in the seventeenth and eighteenth centuries. Its crucial feature was the monopoly of sovereign power it claimed within its territorial limits: there could be only a single such sovereign institution, namely, the state. Only the state could have the power to make laws, to administer punishment, to declare war. Instead of the plethora of authorities with overlapping jurisdictions and the complex web of relations of lordship and subordination that characterized the medieval order, there arose in the nineteenth century the idea of nationhood and of the sovereignty of the people. The modern sovereign nation-state emerged in its fully developed form. Needless to say, in the seventeenth or eighteenth century, only the states of Europe recognized each other's sovereignty. They would make treaties and mark each other's boundaries on maps in order to put the seal of mutual approval on each other's sovereign territorial limits. A refusal to recognize sovereignty or a violation of agreed borders could lead to war. Every war was followed by a new treaty with new lines drawn on the map. Those who had the misfortune to study the diplomatic history of Europe in college will remember the sleepless nights spent trying to memorize the unpronounceable names of remote provinces that were transferred on who knows which dates from one European power to another. That is how we were taught to relish the sublime beauties of sovereignty.

When Europeans went overseas to found their empires, they were of course scarcely concerned about whether they were violating the sovereignty of the conquered countries. In many cases, they would declare quite blatantly that in those uncivilized parts of the world, there was no international law; the only law that prevailed there was the law of force and conquest. Reading the history of imperialism, Indians bled within themselves while asking: "Why could we not protect our sovereignty? Was it not because we failed to defend our sovereignty that we had to face so much misery and humiliation?" All streams within the national movement sought that one goal: to build the independent sovereign national state. This was true not only of the modern history of India but also of every colonized country of Asia, Africa, and the Americas. This was the principal event in international history after World War II. What was the special right only of European nations was now recognized as the universal and fundamental right to self-determination of every nation in the world. Except for Antarctica, every territorial space in the globe was recognized as part of the sovereign jurisdiction of one or the other nation-state.

India's sovereignty has been earned at much cost. Not even in our worst nightmare can we Indians think of giving it up. Europeans look at us a little patronizingly and say, "Well, you've only just become independent, which is why you think there is nothing more precious than sovereignty. But we have seen its good as well as its bad side.

After two world wars, we have realized that loosening the structure of national sovereignty is not such a bad idea after all. It can lead to a lot of good. You will do well to think about it."

The most radical proposals on government and citizenship that attempt to move beyond the limits of the nation-state are coming from Europe. In fact, the European Union routinely curtails the sovereignty of its member nation-states on many matters of law, administration, and the judicial process. A common European currency is now in circulation. Every member-state will have to accept a common constitutional framework for its government. There are now virtually no regulatory controls of the nation-state over matters such as trade, travel, and employment across national borders within Europe. This is not to say that there is complete unanimity on how tight the union should be; no one is saying that the English, the French, and the Germans will completely merge into one political body. The question is not whether the European nation-states will disappear and a federated structure of Europe emerge in its place. Rather, the question is whether the modern historical axiom that the nation-state is the only legitimate site of sovereignty is being abandoned in Europe. Those who speak of radically new notions of sovereignty say, "Yes, that is exactly what is happening, and indeed there should be more of it, not only in Europe but elsewhere too. Because what is happening in Europe is not merely the emergence of a federated structure at the top, but also a loosening of structures below the nation-state. Look how easily Scotland and Wales got their own parliaments. Even thirty years ago, this would have led to civil war."

The new liberal theorists add that alongside sovereignty, notions of citizenship are also undergoing radical change. The idea that the nation-state is the only true home of the citizen, the only guarantor of his or her rights and the only legitimate object of his or her loyalty, is, the new theorists claim, changing fast, and should change even more quickly. In Europe today, it is easy to find a person from one country working in another country, owning a house in a third country, and having the right to vote in all three. One would suppose that this is only natural under globalization. Yet, although such things happen every day in India and Bangladesh and Nepal and Sri Lanka, we don't think of them as natural; on the contrary, we complain and say, "Look, people from other countries are voting in our elections. Stop them." The European liberal will say to us: if we can release the idea of citizenship from the prison of the nation-state and distribute it among different kinds of political affiliations, then we would have the means to deal more effectively, and more democratically, with problems like the rights of migrants, the rights of minorities, cultural diversity within the nation and the freedom of the individual. There will then be little scope for separatism, terror and civil war.

Of course, we on our part could respond to these arguments. We could say that the concepts of sovereignty and citizenship have been loosened so easily in Europe because of the very peculiar historical conditions prevailing there today—conditions that do not exist anywhere else in the world. The history of Western Europe in the second half of the twentieth century is a history of unparalleled prosperity, democratic governance and peace. For more than half a century, there has not been war between the countries of Europe; there is not even the possibility of war. Such a situation is unprecedented in the history of Europe. But the essential condition for this was the cooperation between European and American capital and the mutual roles of the United States and the Soviet Union in the context of the cold war. There has been no war in Europe in the last fifty years because any war would have led to a nuclear exchange. There was no alternative to peace. This created the condition in which experiments with economic and political cooperation could proceed a long way. The concept of national sovereignty has become loose because the states of Europe did not have to face the most difficult tests of sovereignty. They have been able to assume that no European state will ever go to war on its own, certainly not against any other European state. Each state has made its own calculations on how much it will benefit by giving up a little more of its sovereignty in exchange for greater cooperation; the results are often different for each state and, as I have said before, there is no unanimity in this matter. There are many arguments and disputes over specific measures. What is significant is that the question is no longer posed in abstract terms such as the end of sovereignty or fragmented citizenship. There has never been a question of making any general decision of principle. Every debate has taken place over concrete proposals and decisions have been made by each member state after evaluating its specific costs and benefits.

There is little doubt that one of the reasons why notions of global society, global democracy etc. appear so frequently in the writings of European theorists is the tremendous persuasive power of that cherished ideal of liberal politics—an almost utopian dream—that it is possible to resolve all differences and disputes by mutual discussion, negotiation, and the adoption of institutionalized rules and without the use of force. In this imagined world—an ideal generalization of today's Europe—no one will threaten violence, leave the negotiation table and pick up weapons, amass guns and troops at the borders, or send bombers into someone else's skies. These assumptions are now virtually taken for granted in Europe. Sovereignty has been loosened in Europe with the acquiescence of the nation-states, not in opposition to their wishes. The state in Europe does not fear a breach of the peace, because the guarantor of peace in Europe is not any of the European nation-states. That guarantor is the United States, the world's only superpower. It is under the supervision of that great power that there prevails in Europe today the great peace. Another name for the great peace is empire.

IV

Indians know empire only too well. As a result, when we see the dominance of the United States in the world today, most of us have little trouble in recognizing it as empire. Yet it is necessary to understand that compared to the empires we have heard of in history, the present American empire is quite fundamentally of a different character.

Empire in modern world history has meant conquest of foreign lands, establishing dominion over them, including them within one's own territorial realm. If there was a competing empire, the rivalry was over how much territory each empire had conquered. Austria, Russia, and Turkey had territorial empires in Europe. Spain, Portugal, Britain, France, and Holland had empires overseas. All empires came to an end in the second half of the twentieth century. As I have said before, that was the age of the self-determination of nations and the sovereignty of the people. That was also the age of the competing dominance of U.S. and Soviet power, resulting in the cold war. Many who studied the nature of the capitalist system in those decades characterized it as neocolonialism. Americans did not like the description. The U.S. republic was founded following a revolution against an empire; it was there that the sovereignty of the people was first enshrined in a constitution. Naturally, Americans were stung when they were called imperialists.

The last ten years have changed everything. Now in the United States, politicians, journalists and policymakers are saying quite openly, "Let us face the facts. This is empire. So we better get rid of old and hackneyed ideas and decide how best to run it." It is not only those on the conservative Right who are saying this. In fact, they are saying it much less than others, because many on the Right are still coming to grips with the ways of the new global politics. It is liberals who are the most vocal about the new empire. What is most interesting is that the Italian Marxist revolutionary and theorist Antonio Negri and his American collaborator Michael Hardt have also written at length on the new empire.[8]

What is this new empire? Well, this empire does not conquer territory, or impose its own administration or taxes on the defeated country. It does not even send its armed forces to battle unless it becomes absolutely necessary. This empire is democratic. It acknowledges the sovereignty of the people. Is it the case then that the people of one country are exercising sovereignty over the people of another? That is old-fashioned nineteenth-century colonialism. What is so new about that? Well, it turns out that is not quite the case. When thousands of missiles flew in from American warships and reduced the city of Belgrade to rubble, no one thought that the people of the United States were about to claim sovereignty over the people of Serbia. In fact, when the Serbian government accepted defeat in war, no one on the American side thought that there would now be an American administration in Serbia, that the American flag would fly from its capital, or that American soldiers would patrol the streets of

Belgrade. In fact, the main concern was to bring back the American troops as quickly as possible. This new empire has no rival empire to compete against. Empire is global. Under its realm, one state does not exercise sovereignty over another. It is empire that is sovereign.

Some European liberal writers are saying that Immanuel Kant's dream, described in the eighteenth-century age of enlightenment, is now about to come true. While acknowledging the fact that each state would act according to its own laws and interests, Kant nevertheless speculated that if a single universal, rational, and supreme code of international practice could be established throughout the world, then perpetual peace was possible. Liberals are now saying that the time has come to establish such a globally applicable code of practice. International law and basic human rights must be established all over the world. Where these are violated, the guilty must be punished, without undue regard for the privileges of national sovereignty. If the leaders of states themselves have little concern for the law, if they themselves ride roughshod over the human rights of people, then why should the excuse of national sovereignty be allowed to come to their rescue? In that case, human rights would never be established. What is needed, therefore, is the drafting of a global code of state practice and the creation of international institutions to monitor and implement this code. On what authority will these international judicial institutions be set up? Bodies run on the principle of one-country-one-vote, such as the United Nations General Assembly, will be utterly inadequate for the task. The liberal democratic countries must come forward to accept their responsibility in creating the institutional space for the operation of an ideal global sovereignty. The name for this sovereign sphere, I have said before, is empire.

Of course, there are many in Europe and the United States who are not liberals. They do not dream of the establishment of human rights all over the world. They call themselves realists. They have no doubt in their minds about the overwhelming role of national interest and national power in international politics. But even they have begun to realize the attractions of empire. The reason for this is that the first and most important function of empire is to maintain the peace. The cold war days of peace through the mutual balance of terror are gone. Who has the ability now to maintain peace in the world? The only legitimate, rational, universally acknowledged power that can establish a regime of peace throughout the world is the sovereign empire. This empire will not go to war. It has no rival, no enemies; against whom will it go to war? It will use its military power only to maintain peace. In other words, instead of going to war, the armed forces of empire will police the whole world. If necessary, they will use force— after all, the police too must use force—but legitimately, within the law, to establish the rule of law. It will exercise only as much force as necessary. Just as the police are blamed for applying excessive force, the same rule must apply to the forces of empire. We need to keep in mind that the American public today is unprepared to accept the death of American soldiers in overseas military action. They regard Saddam Hussein or Milosevic as thugs and criminals, not as enemies of the American nation. To deal with thugs and criminals, one has to send out the police to arrest and imprison them; one does not expect the police to lay down their lives for the country. The American armed forces are now preparing to act as the police force of the world. Only a few American soldiers died in the war in the Persian Gulf, and probably none in the war in Serbia.

Most people, even those who have no particular liking for the policies of the United States or even for the West, are agreed that the first task of empire is to maintain the peace. Take the case of the conflict between Israel and Palestine on which people from both sides will argue that there is no possibility of a peaceful solution, or of even a serious peace proposal, without the active backing of the United States. There are new conflicts emerging every day in the fragments that once constituted the former Yugoslavia. In each case, one hears of the need for international intervention, which means initially European troops and, if that does not work, American bombers, American missiles, American troops. Even on the Kashmir dispute, which has remained unresolved for over fifty years, one hears from both Indian and Pakistani spokespersons that the outlines of a solution are clear and obvious; all one needs is a sovereign power that can force the two sides to sit at the table and sign the agreement. The only trouble is that the leaders of empire are so busy elsewhere that they can't find the time to even look in that direction.

The theorists of the new empire have talked of still more wonderful things. This empire is democratic. It is an empire without an emperor. The people are sovereign here, as it should be in a democracy. That is precisely the reason why this empire has no geographical limits. This is not like the empires of old where new territories have to be conquered by war to add to the size of the empire. Now empire expands because more and more people, and even governments, looking for peace and the lure of economic prosperity, want to come under its sheltering umbrella. Thus, empire does not conquer territory or destroy property; rather, it encompasses new countries within its web of power, makes room for them in its network. The key to empire is not force but control. There is always a limit to force; there is no limit to control. Hence, empire's vision is a global democracy.

We can see the exercise of control right in front of our eyes. I have earlier talked about the global control that can be now exercised over national economies because of economic and financial globalization. The attempt to rewrite international commercial and trade laws and to set up new institutions to enforce them is proceeding rapidly. Even such a deeply political matter as punishment for alleged violations of human rights has now become the jurisdiction of new international judicial institutions. The trial of Milosevic is the most dramatic example of this. Liberals hope that other equally important and notorious violators of human rights will be brought before such international trial courts. There is a new law in Belgium that says that any violation of human rights in any country of the world can be brought for trial before a Belgian court. Four persons have been recently convicted under this law for involvement in the genocide in Rwanda. There is a bizarre irony in the fact that Belgium, which only a hundred years ago supervised one of the world's most brutal colonial regimes in the Congo, should now claim the right to try any human rights violator anywhere in the world. But these are only the most glaring examples. If the protection of human rights is a function of empire, then that task is being carried out not simply by the international courts. It is being done daily, and diligently, by numerous such international NGOs as Amnesty International, Médicins sans Frontières, or Oxfam, whose able and committed activists probably have never suspected that they are, like little squirrels, carrying the sand and pebbles that go into the building of the great bridgehead of empire.[9] But that is where the ideological foundations of empire are being laid.

We have, then, a global and sovereign empire. But let me remind you once more: that it will be a mistake to think of the sovereignty of this empire within the old model of national sovereignty. This empire is not claiming proprietorship over the territory of the entire globe. It recognizes the principle that each country and its inhabitants should be ruled by governments that are representative of the people of that country. It does not demand that every country must have the same constitution or the same administrative system. It is not claiming some kind of political homogeneity all over the globe. Its key principle is control, not occupation or appropriation. In its nature, empire today is consistent with the transformed character of capital.

Analyzing the nature of modern industrial capital in the nineteenth century, Marx showed how, despite the incidental and transient incorporation of many elements of the precapitalist production system within the new capitalist network of circulation of commodities, the historical tendency was toward the inevitable collapse of precapitalist production and the rise of properly capitalist production. Distinguishing between the two stages, Marx called the former stage that of the formal, and the latter the real, subsumption of labor to capital. A century and a half after Marx, many theorists describing the present character of capital are pointing out that capital no longer demands that all production must take place in large factories with assembly lines. In fact, many commodities that were produced in the large factories of advanced industrial countries only thirty years ago are now being manufactured under the supervision of multinational companies virtually as cottage industries in third world villages. Given a new conglomeration of factors such as new technologies, the managerial reorganization of capitalist firms, new techniques of control of labor by capital, the expansion of financial instruments and credit mechanisms, etc. capital today is far more flexible than before. It can now accommodate far greater variation and hybridity than it did fifty or a hundred years ago. It has learnt to get along with many techniques and practices that belong to precapitalist traditions. Today, one may find in many advanced capitalist organizations that workers have no fixed hours of work, that they may take a lot of work home, or work twelve or fourteen hours a day in order to earn more. One of the consequences of globalization is that for the first time after the industrial revolution, such huge numbers of unorganized laborers, especially women, from all over the world are coming under the productive sway of large-scale capital. When reading the history of the industrial revolution, we were once told that the factory laws that regulated maximum hours of work or minimum wages were enacted to promote the long-term expansion of capital. Capital today, seeking new frontiers of growth, is beginning to think of those laws as shackles imposed by history. Even when it is not possible entirely to throw them away, it seems prudent sometimes to wriggle out of their grasp.

Thus, flexible capital combines with flexible sovereignty to produce empire that is flexible enough to adjust itself to conjunctural and local situations and to thus devise new and appropriate forms of governance. The theorists of the new empire, whether conservative, liberal, or leftist, assert that this is the only way to establish and hold the peace in today's world. Among political leaders, perhaps not everyone is equally convinced of this new reality. During the Clinton administration, it often appeared as though there was a conscious policy of directing such an empire. Liberals complain about the present Bush administration that it is still mired in the old thinking of the cold war era and is insufficiently attentive to the changed realities and needs of the present world.

I will conclude by raising some issues that are recently agitating leftist thinkers around the world. Many writers belonging to the Left are so vociferous these days about establishing universal human rights that it is difficult to distinguish them from run-of-the-mill liberals. During the war in Serbia, there was often little difference between their thinking and the statements put out by NATO spokesmen. Some leftist writers are, however, talking of going beyond the framework of the sovereign nation-state to create wider and deeper democratic forms of government. But their ideas are still limited to Europe. I have already said that in the unique situation of Europe, it is easy to think of shedding the straitjacket of national sovereignty. Elsewhere, it is much more difficult to treat the sovereignty of the nation-state so lightly. The most novel proposal has been made by Antonio Negri who says that just as capital today is unlike the industrial capital of the nineteenth or twentieth centuries, so is empire today quite unlike the imperialism described by Lenin. Today, the idea that the organized industrial working class would lead the struggle against capital is completely implausible. Similarly, the idea that the interest of the national bourgeoisie and the sovereignty of the nation-state in the third world must be defended in the struggle against imperialism is equally doomed to failure. Globalization cannot be fought with the legal powers of the nation-state. What is needed is to devise new revolutionary strategies that are appropriate for the age of globalization. Negri says: the exploited all over the world must demand not only universal human rights but universal citizenship. If capital can be global, if sovereignty can claim to be global, then why cannot workers demand the right to look for work, to settle down and exercise citizenship, in any country of the world? Only such a demand, Negri claims, will throw a truly revolutionary challenge to global capital as well as to empire.

Of course, political strategies cannot be derived in this way as though they were theorems of geometry. Negri's dream that multitudes around the world, through their unorganized struggles, will one day spontaneously destroy the foundations of global capital will seem to us, many times defeated in thoughtless battles, as little more than a hopeful tale told on a rainy day. Hardt and Negri's celebration of the supposedly radical break between the old order of industrial capital and national sovereignty and the new reality of global empire without a center is, without doubt, hasty and starry-eyed. Yet we should not for that reason ignore what the theorists of globalization are telling us—that it is impossible to avoid its global tentacles by putting up walls around the national economy. What is needed, therefore, is an adequate response to the flexible strategies of rule adopted by empire—an equally flexible, mixed, and variable anti-empire politics. "Away with globalization" is not a very clever slogan; but equally foolish and unrealistic is the desire to let oneself be swept away by every global current. We hear the former slogan from both the Right and the Left in India. And the latter tendency we see every day in the print media and on television. As far as the leaders of the Indian government are concerned, they appear to have so profoundly understood the intricate mysteries of empire that they have prostrated themselves in Washington in order to be appointed the provincial governor of this region of Asia. Needless to say, questions such as the global dominance of capital or the interests of laborers or the struggle of the oppressed are not relevant questions for them. They say, American hegemony today is unchallenged; it is only wise to cooperate.

What is peculiar is that the more empire takes the shape of an unchallenged sovereign hegemony, the more the world resists. These days, whenever leaders of Western governments or the captains of multinational companies or the directors of international financial institutions try to assemble somewhere for a meeting, thousands of demonstrators gather in the city and demonstrate, often managing to disrupt the official program. This has happened recently in the cities of Europe and North America, without any central organization, apparently spontaneously. It would be silly to say that these demonstrations are shaking the foundations of either capital or empire, although the demonstrators are likely to leave behind a few scratches and dents. But there is no doubt that because of globalization large sections of people are losing control over their environment and ways of life. Control is being centralized in the headquarters of capital and empire, over which no one has any control, because the officials are not elected by any body of citizens, nor are they accountable to any representative institution. This is the principal contradiction of empire today. The empire stands by democracy; yet so far it has not presented any framework of global democracy. Hence, although most people defer to the reality of empire's power, there is no moral legitimacy to its dominance. Quoting the phrase coined by Ranajit Guha, one of Professor Susobhan Sarkar's most distinguished students, we could say that this is "dominance without hegemony."[10] Like all empires, this one too will one day collapse. Its crisis will deepen precisely over the question of democracy—over the struggles, now being carried out in different parts of the world, to broaden and deepen the practices of democracy.

FIVE

Battle Hymn

I consider the attacks carried out in this city on September 11 as heinous and barbaric. I am not one of those who proclaim political nonviolence. As a student of politics in colonial and postcolonial countries, I have become convinced that when the structures of domination in the modern world are so deeply rooted in the ability to deploy massive and efficient violence, it is neither possible nor justified to insist that those who fight against unfair domination must at all times eschew the use of political violence. But I know of no anti-imperialist or anti-colonial politics that will justify the killing of five thousand ordinary men and women in a deliberate act of violence against a civilian target. Even if, by some contorted political logic, one were to think that one was at war with the United States, it would be a hard act to justify, even as an act of war. I believe that such deliberate and calculated acts of massive terror have emerged out of a politics and an ideology that are fundamentally mistaken and that must be rejected and condemned. Such ideologies of religious or ethnic fanaticism are widespread today and they are by no means restricted to any one religious community. I am one of those who argue that we must sympathetically understand the reasons why so many people all over the world are persuaded by such ideologies of fanat-

Text of talk at meeting organized by students of Columbia University in New York on September 21, 2001.

icism. However, that is not to say that we must sympathize with or endorse their politics.

Having said that, let me turn to the question of the response to these acts of terror. Within hours of the event, the President of the United States announced that his country was at war. Immediately, the analogy was being drawn to Pearl Harbor. Not since World War II, we were told, had America been attacked in this way. I have been asking ever since, why was it necessary to make that announcement? How was the determination made so quickly? Was it because war is such a familiar trope in the public memory of Western countries? From fiction to history books to the cinema, there are innumerable sources of popular culture in the West that have taught people what war means and what one ought to do when one's country goes to war. We saw it in this country last week when people flew the flag, lined up to donate blood or sang the *Battle Hymn of the Republic* in memorial services in church. An unprecedented act of violence was made comprehensible by framing it as an act of war. Perhaps George W. Bush, inexperienced in the affairs of state, was closer to the popular understanding than the seasoned veterans of the State Department when he said that he wanted Osama bin Laden "dead or alive." Revenge and retaliation are also familiar sentiments of war. So when President Bush said, albeit within his somewhat limited political vocabulary, that he would "smoke 'em out and hunt 'em down," he was using a rhetoric long familiar in the American national language of warfare.

It is now clear that by declaring a war so quickly, the U.S. decisionmakers have found themselves pushed into a corner from which they are having a hard time getting out. Ten days after the attack, there has been no visible military response. Experts are trying to tell people that this is not a conventional enemy; it has no country, no territory, no borders. There are no obvious targets that could be attacked. It could take a long time to build an international coalition and strike effectively at the enemy. This is not a war against a country or a people. It is a war against terrorism. But having been told that this was a war, the people are dismayed by the lack of any recognizable response. There is a virtual volcano of rage and frustration that has built up in this country. The people are in no mood for metaphorical wars. They are, if I may use some plain language too, baying for blood.

In the absence of a clear enemy or target, the rhetoric is frequently slipping into unconcealed religious, ethnic, and cultural hatred. And it is not mere rhetoric either, because there have been attacks on mosques and temples, assaults on foreign-looking men and women, and at least two killings. Senior leaders, including the President, have attempted to reassure Arab-Americans that their safety will not be jeopardized. And yet the rhetoric of cultural intolerance continues. Responsible leaders speak on radio and television of what must be done with the uncivilized parts of the world, of keeping a close watch on neighbors with Arabic names and of people who "wear diapers around their heads." They speak of "ending" states like Afghanistan, Iraq, Syria, and Libya and "finishing off" Islamic militants in Lebanon and Palestine. If this is how the elite speaks, can we blame ordinary people for making sense of this war as a conflict of civilizations?

We can and should, I think, ask questions about responsibility and accountability. If the war on terrorism is a war unlike any other this country has fought, as we are now being told, that should have been clear from the first day. Why then mislead everyone by invoking the familiar language of retaliation against enemy countries and enemy peoples? If the United States is indeed the only superpower in a new world without borders, the cultural resources of traditional war will be singularly inadequate and inappropriate for that new imperial role. Has the leadership acted responsibly in preparing both itself and the country for such a role?

There is another huge question of responsibility concerning America's role in the rest of the world. Given its overwhelming military and economic dominance, every action by the United States in any part of the world cannot but have enormous repercussions on those states and societies. Has America acted responsibly in weighing the long-term, and often unintended, consequences of its actions? I will not speak here of the Middle East, for instance, where American policy has had enormous historical impact. Let me speak of Afghanistan where, in the early 1980s, the United States fought a long proxy war against the Soviet Union. It is said to have been the biggest CIA operation in history. The United States, in collaboration with the military regime in Pakistan and the conservative monarchy of Saudi Arabia, organized, trained, funded and armed the Afghan militants, encouraged their Islamic ideology and applauded when they successfully drove out the Soviet troops. I heard Zbigniew Bzrezinski, a familiar figure in the corridors of Columbia University, say on television last night that when the last Soviet soldiers crossed the Amu Daria back into the Soviet Union, he felt very very good. He also said that he would have felt even better had he known at the time that that would be the beginning of the collapse of the Soviet Union. I don't suppose he even thought for a moment the disastrous consequences the American involvement would have on the region. The Taliban was born in the 1980s in the mujahideen camps in Pakistan. Osama bin Laden became a hero of Islamic militancy at that time. The Pakistani army itself became deeply afflicted by the ideology of Islamic fanaticism. The results are now there for all to see. Has the United States ever accepted that it has some responsibility for what was done to the region and what the region is now doing to the rest of the world?

The question should be asked today when battleships, bombers, and commando troops are taking up positions for military operations. Is anyone thinking what might be the consequences of another war in Afghanistan? The consequences for Pakistan? The consequences for all of South Asia where there are two countries with nuclear weapons and a political atmosphere seething in religious and sectarian conflict?

Like it or not, comprehend it or not, the United States is today the world's only imperial power. As such, everything it does has consequences for all the world. It is not only the collateral damage of military action that American defense analysts must think of. American leaders must also necessarily think of the collateral damage they do to the history of societies and peoples all over the world. If the United States is the world's only superpower, it must be responsible for its actions to the people of the whole world.

I am not persuaded that either the American leadership or the American people are aware of the enormous moral responsibility contemporary history has put on them. In the aftermath of the attacks on the World Trade Center, President Bush could only think of the "Wanted" poster he had seen in Western movies. While the whole world is looking for an American policy that is flexible, sensitive, attuned to the enormous changes that have taken place in the world in the last decade or so, what we will probably get is more of the familiar American arrogance, bludgeoning, and insensitivity. Perhaps, sadly, the first war of the twenty-first century will end up no differently from the many wars of the twentieth.

SIX

The Contradictions of Secularism

I

In view of all that has happened in different parts of South Asia in recent months, it is not easy for us at this moment to apply the cold logic of analytical reasoning and talk dispassionately about the prospects of secularism. It is not a time of normal politics in South Asian countries. In some, Afghanistan for example, civil war and external military intervention have uprooted previously existing political structures. Politics there is still being transacted through warfare and it is too early to tell whether stable foundations are being laid for a new political order. We are told that in Pakistan, there is a grim struggle between a general who wants to lead his country into membership of the exclusive club of liberal democracies and die-hard fundamentalists who want to create their own brand of Islamic society. There is enough reason for us to believe that the real story of contemporary Pakistan is far more complicated than that. In Nepal, a bizarre massacre in the royal palace has been followed by virtually full-scale war between security forces and Maoist rebels. In Sri Lanka, there appears to have been a new breakthrough in bringing peace to a country torn by prolonged and violent ethnic conflict. But such hopes have been dashed so often in the past that it would be rash to predict that there will be normal politics in Sri Lanka in the near future. Even Bangla-

Closing address delivered at the Conference on "Siting Secularism" at Oberlin College, Oberlin, Ohio on April 21, 2002.

desh, where religious conflict in the political arena is rare, saw a spate of attacks on the minority community following the recent elections; fortunately, timely intervention by civic and political groups managed to contain the damage. In several parts of northern and western India, however, and in Gujarat in particular, attacks on the minority community reached such a horrifying scale of organized violence that the very idea of a constitutional state guaranteeing the physical safety of all its citizens has been put under threat. I do not believe that I am being unduly alarmist in suggesting that a new element has now entered the arena of what is being regarded as legitimate politics in India. It is the idea, now being voiced not from the extremist fringes but from the very center of representative institutions, that the constitutionally guaranteed rights of minorities must be negotiated afresh in the political domain. This has put the question of secularism in India in a new, emotionally charged, context.

There is one more new element that has become relevant in recent months. Following the events of September 11, the United States has adopted a new imperial role in world politics by claiming to be conducting a worldwide war of terrorism. This is not the place for me to analyze the connection between the so-called war on terrorism and the utterly cynical pursuit of what the present administration thinks to be the American national interest. But there have been at least two immediate consequences for the politics of secularism in South Asian countries. One is the new legitimacy that has been given to legal instruments that curtail civil liberties on the grounds of national security and the fight against terrorism. In India, for example, new laws have been passed for detention without trial and expanded methods of surveillance. The results of long years of struggle by the civil liberties and democratic rights movement were nullified at one stroke. Spokesmen for the government were able to claim with aplomb that if liberal democracies like the United States and Britain could have new laws to fight terrorism, why can't we? The second, and more subtle, effect comes from the new complex of meanings that has suddenly congealed around the term "terrorist." Faced with repeated questions, American political leaders continue to insist that the war on terrorism is not a war on Islam. And yet, given the utter lack of political clarity or consistency about the meaning of terrorism, accompanied by the cynical pursuit of realist political goals by the United States, most people have drawn their own conclusions about who can be called a terrorist in these tumultuous times. There is a new ring of legitimacy, for instance, to the recent accusation made by the leader of a Hindu right-wing organization who said, "All Muslims may not be terrorists, but most terrorists are Muslims."[1] There was a time when such a remark would have been dismissed as absurd. Not any more, because it now appears to have a global sanction. Even the Prime Minister of India, speaking at the recent conference of the ruling Bharatiya Janata Party in Goa, said roughly the same thing.

There is much in our present situation, therefore, to make us feel outraged, angry and agitated. Nevertheless, I accept that we, as professional social scientists and analysts, have a responsibility to continue the debates over secularism within the accepted forms of scientific discourse. To do this, I have chosen to move away from the battlefields of Afghanistan, Pakistan, or Gujarat to the relatively calmer regions of eastern India. My intuition is that by focusing on a place like West Bengal, ruled for the last twenty-five years by a communist-led Left Front government, we might be able to talk usefully about the conditions for a democratic politics of secularism. I want to concentrate in particular on ways of handling what I think are the contradictions within the politics of secularism in India.

II

In an essay published a few years ago, I had identified what seemed to me two contradictions of the politics of secularism in India.[2] First, although a significant section of Indian political leaders shared the desire to separate the domains of religion and politics, the independent Indian state, for various historical reasons, had no option but to involve itself in the regulation, funding and, in some cases, even the administration of various religious institutions. Second, even as sections of Indian citizens were legally demarcated as belonging to minority religious communities following their own personal laws and having the right to establish and administer their own educational institutions, there was no procedure to determine who was to represent these minority communities in their dealings with the state.

The politics of secularism and communalism has gone through a turbulent history in India in the last two decades. But I do not think these two contradictions have been overcome or resolved. I continue to hold that the conditions for a more democratic politics of secularism cannot be created unless we grapple with these contradictions. The task is by no means easy, as I will show by discussing a recent episode from West Bengal that was labeled by the media as the "madrasah controversy."

On January 19, 2002, speaking at a public meeting in Siliguri, Buddhadeb Bhattacharya, chief minister of West Bengal, said that there were many madrasahs (Muslim religious schools) not affiliated with the West Bengal Madrasah Board where anti-national terrorists, including operatives of the Pakistan intelligence agency, were active. These unauthorized madrasahs would have to be shut down. This remark, however, might not have had the effect it did if a major incident had not happened in Calcutta three days later.

On January 22, 2002, in the early hours of the morning, two motorbikes drove up in front of the American Center in Calcutta. The policemen on security duty there were changing shifts at the time. Suddenly, the pillion riders on the motorbikes pulled out automatic rifles and began to shoot. The policemen were apparently so taken aback by this unexpected attack that they were unable to respond. After forty seconds during which the two riflemen fired more than sixty rounds of bullets, the motorbikes sped away leaving five policemen dead and several others injured. The incident immediately made international headlines and the first presumption was that it was another attack by Islamic terrorists against the United States. It later transpired that the attack had been launched by a criminal gang based in Dubai, seeking revenge for the death of one of its associates in an encounter with the police. But the criminal network overlapped with that of suspected Islamic militants operating in different parts of India. One of the first suspects arrested in connection with the killings was a mathematics teacher of a madrasah in North 24-Parganas, from a place about thirty miles north of Calcutta. He was said to be a member of SIMI, the banned Islamic students' organization. Another madrasah teacher, said to be a Bangladeshi national with connections to the Pakistani intelligence services, was arrested in Murshidabad district.

On January 24, speaking to the press in Calcutta, Buddhadeb Bhattacharya clarified his earlier remarks and said, "Certain madrasahs, not all madrasahs—I repeat, certain madrasahs—are involved in anti-national propaganda. We have definite information on this. This cannot be allowed." Four days later, at a public meeting at Domkal in Murshidabad, he said that all madrasahs would have to seek affiliation with the Madrasah Board. "We will not allow unaffiliated madrasahs to run here," he said. He instructed the district administration to carry out a survey of all madrasahs in Murshidabad and report on the number of students, teachers, boarders, and sources of funding.[3]

The chief minister's comments, as reported in the press, immediately ignited a controversy. It was alleged that by suggesting a police surveillance of madrasahs, the chief minister had maligned the entire Muslim community of West Bengal. If there were specific allegations against particular institutions, the offenders should be punished, but why should an entire system of minority educational institutions be tarred with the same brush? Madrasah students, demonstrating in Calcutta, demanded that the chief minister apologize. The students said that madrasah teachers were being harassed and that an atmosphere of witch hunt had been created because of "misinformation and poor understanding" of the system of madrasah education. It was reported that the Urdu press was comparing Bhattacharya not only with Hindu right-wing leaders like L. K. Advani and Bal Thackeray but also with "Musharraf, the military dictator of Pakistan."[4] The protests came not only from those who claimed to speak on behalf of Muslim organizations or from the opposition political parties, but also from partners of the ruling Left Front. Several Front leaders said that the chief minister's remarks sounded alarmingly like those of BJP leaders in Delhi and that this would send wrong signals to the minority com-

munity in the state. In fact, an emergency meeting of the Left Front
was called on February 6 to clarify the government's position.[5]

On January 31, the state Minority Commission organized a meeting of Muslim intellectuals and academics at which Mohammed
Salim, the Communist Party of India (Marxist) (CPI[M]) minister
for minority affairs, explained that the chief minister had not made
a blanket allegation against all madrasahs and that there was not going
to be any witch hunt. In fact, he praised the initiative taken by community leaders to set up madrasahs. "These institutions are a national
asset. It is laudable that some individuals or organizations have
reached remote rural areas to spread some sort of education even
before the government could open a school there." But he defended
the chief minister by saying that the government must take steps
against "anti-national and communal forces along the Indo-Bangla
border as the area has become a second front for anti-Indian forces.
Terrorism is not religion-specific. There will be a crackdown irrespective of whether it is a madrasah, mosque, temple or club."[6]

Nevertheless, there continued to be reports that Muslims were
agitated about what they regarded as an unprovoked accusation
against an entire community of complicity with terrorism. They alleged that several teachers of madrasahs had been picked up by the
police after the American Center killings and later released because
of lack of evidence against them.[7] The police, it was alleged, was proceeding on the basis of certain preconceived and unsubstantiated ste-
reotypes. There were even reports from several places in the border
districts of North 24-Parganas and Nadia that Communist Party
members belonging to the minority community were alarmed that
the chief minister's remarks sounded so much like those of the BJP
home minister Advani. "Such statements from the chief minister will
only encourage the terrorists as they will get a fertile ground among
the irate Muslims to spread their organization," said Waris Sheikh
who had been with the Communist Party for forty years.[8] On February 4, a surprisingly large rally organized in Calcutta by the Jamiat-
e-Ulema-e-Hind once again demanded a public apology from
Buddhadeb Bhattacharya, this time calling him an agent of the United
States and Israel.[9]

The matter had clearly gone too far. It was announced that the chief minister had called a meeting of Muslim organizations and intellectuals for February 7 where he would explain his position.[10] He also claimed that his remarks in Siliguri had been misquoted by the press and even by the CPI(M) party newspaper *Ganashakti*. At a meeting of the Left Front on February 6, Buddhadeb Bhattacharya was apparently roundly criticized by partners of the Front and even by the former chief minister Jyoti Basu.[11]

By this time, a strategy to handle the fallout appears to have been worked out. The crucial move was to separate the issue of terrorism from that of madrasah education. It was explained that neither the chief minister nor the government had ever suggested that all madrasahs were involved in terrorist propaganda or recruitment. Only when there was specific evidence of such involvement would the government move against particular organizations or individuals, and that too according to the law. The issue of madrasah education was a completely separate matter and the press had misrepresented the chief minister's remarks on this subject by tying it with the question of terrorism. As far as madrasah education was concerned, the Left Front government in West Bengal had done more than any other government in India. Biman Bose, the chairman of the Left Front, explained that in the nearly two hundred years from 1780, when the Alia Madrasah was founded in Calcutta by Warren Hastings, to 1977 when the Left Front came to power, a total of 238 madrasahs had been set up in West Bengal with government approval. Since 1977, in twenty-five years, this number had more than doubled. In 1977, the government expenditure on madrasah education was Rs.500,000; in 2001, it was Rs.1150 million, an increase of more than two thousand times. The entire financial responsibility, including salaries of teachers and supporting staff, of madrasahs affiliated to the state Madrasah Board was borne by the government. Students graduating from affiliated madrasahs in West Bengal were entitled to admission to all universities and all professional courses. This was unprecedented in independent India.[12]

On February 7, the chief minister met a gathering of Muslim leaders and intellectuals, including writers, journalists, teachers, doctors, and imams of mosques. He admitted that his words as reported by the media might have caused confusion and anxiety; he was prepared to share the blame for this and expressed his regret. He reiterated that anti-national elements were active in the state, but clarified that such activities were not confined to madrasahs. Just as there were fundamentalist Hindu organizations, so there were outfits like the Lashkar-e-Taiba that were involved in anti-national and terrorist acts. He had never suggested that all madrasahs were under a cloud of suspicion. There was no legal obligation for madrasahs to seek the approval of the government, and there was no law by which the government could close down private schools, no matter who ran them. "The constitution guarantees minorities the right to run their educational institutions," he said. "Christian missionaries and Hindu organizations are also running their own schools." But the question of modernization of the madrasah curriculum was an urgent issue. The government had appointed a committee headed by Professor A. R. Kidwai, former governor, to look into the matter. "We will try and persuade the unrecognized madrasahs to revise their curricula so that modern subjects could be introduced along with religious studies. We will urge them to join the educational mainstream." He urged Muslim community leaders to think seriously of ways to educate Muslim children so that they had better skills for entry into professional employment and did not become isolated from the rest of the nation. At the end of the meeting, the imams of two leading mosques said that a lot of tension had been created in the past few days over the chief minister's remarks. Some of that communication gap had now been bridged.[13]

The media in general interpreted the chief minister's clarifications as a climb-down forced on him by the adverse reaction both within and outside the party and the Left Front. Several commentators alleged that a courageous initiative to tackle the problem of Islamic fundamentalism from within the parameters of secular politics in India had been stymied because of the relentless pressure of the minority vote bank. Two interesting organizational changes were also reported. First, it was suggested that in view of the misunderstanding and controversy, the affairs of madrasah administration would be taken out of the charge of Kanti Biswas, the school education minister, and given to Mohammed Salim, the minority affairs minister. It was said that Biswas had taken a hard line on madrasah reform and was pushing for the conversion of government-supported senior madrasahs, which provided religious education, to high madrasahs, which followed a strictly secular curriculum. "Why should the government pay the salaries of teachers who provide religious education in madrasahs when it did not do so in other religious schools?" Biswas had apparently asked.[14] The other significant change was within the CPI(M) party daily *Ganashakti*. The chief minister had alleged that his remarks had been misrepresented even in the report published by the party newspaper. Dipen Ghosh, senior trade unionist and former member of parliament, was asked to relinquish his position as editor of the daily and on February 25, Narayan Dutta, a relatively inconspicuous member of the state committee, was appointed in his place.

III

Reconstructing the controversy, both the possibilities and the constraints of a secular state policy on religious minorities in India become apparent. The Left Front in West Bengal, and the CPI(M) in particular, has always proclaimed, with justified pride, that in spite of having a large Muslim minority and a long history of communal conflict until the 1960s, the state has seen undisturbed communal peace in the last twenty-five years. With the exception of a brief outburst, controlled quickly by prompt administrative and political action, in 1992 following the Babari Masjid demolition and attacks on Hindu temples in Bangladesh, there has been no communal riot in West Bengal under Left Front rule. According to most observers of elections in West Bengal, the Left has consistently won the greater part of the Muslim vote. The parties of the Left, and once again the CPI(M) in particular, have recruited leaders from the minority community in several districts. It is likely that many of these young leaders were attracted to the parties of the Left because of their image as secular, modern, and progressive organizations.

Although the issue of modernization of madrasahs suddenly appeared in the public limelight because of its association with the question of terrorism, there is reason to believe that the CPI(M) leadership had been engaged with the issue for some time. Alongside the extension of government financial support to madrasahs affiliated with the Madrasah Board, the Front also initiated in the 1980s a process of change by which the high and junior high madrasahs—some 400 in number—came to follow the same curriculum as regular secondary schools except for a single compulsory course in Arabic. In fact, the point was made during the recent controversy that high madrasahs in the state had significant numbers of non-Muslim students as well as teachers. They also had more female than male students, reflecting the fact that many Muslim families felt more comfortable sending their daughters to madrasahs rather than to regular secondary schools. Teachers were recruited through the same School Service Commission that chose teachers for all other secondary schools. The 100-odd senior madrasahs, also affiliated to the Madrasah Board and financially supported by the government, followed a revised curriculum in which about two-thirds of courses consisted of English, Bengali, physical and life sciences, mathematics, history, and geography and about one-third of courses on Islamic religion and law. It was alleged that senior madrasahs had become an anomaly because they did not prepare their students adequately for either the religious or the secular professions. There were fewer and fewer students, those wanting a religious education preferring to go to one of the many private madrasahs outside the Madrasah Board system.[15] There was a renewed initiative now to further modernize the madrasah curriculum. A committee had been set up with Professor A. R. Kidwai as chairman, to look into the matter. Kidwai himself, in an interview given during the recent controversy, suggested that traditional Yunani medicine and modern Arabic might be introduced into the madrasahs to make their curricula more suitable for new employment opportunities.[16]

Nonetheless, it remains a fact that the involvement of nonaffiliated madrasahs with the activities and propaganda of militant Islamic groups began to worry the party leadership even before the American

Centre killings. It was not merely because there were police intelligence reports suggesting such involvement. The Muslim leaders of the party themselves became aware of the impact that fundamentalist propaganda was producing in Muslim neighborhoods. A striking example was provided by Anisur Rahaman, a CPI(M) minister, in an op-ed article in *Ganashakti*.[17] Entitled "Fasting for Laden," the article describes the leader's visit to a Muslim village where he is told that people were observing a fast. Surprised, because the month of Ramadan was a long time away, he asks the villagers what the fast was for. The villagers explain that they were praying for the safety of Osama bin Laden who had been made the target of attack by the imperialist Americans. The meeting that the minister had come to address began late in the evening after everyone had broken the fast. The rest of the article is a summary of the speech of a certain Rahman Chacha, a village elder, who makes several arguments, having to do with political ethics as well as tactics, on why Muslims in India had no reason to support bin Laden. The fact that these arguments were presented in the voice of a nonpolitical "wise man" of the community and not in that of the communist minister himself is interesting. But the most striking thing about the article was its recognition of the impact that a few "hot-headed and thoughtless young men" were having on many ordinary Muslims.

The most contentious issue, of course, was that of the private madrasahs that everyone agreed were growing rapidly in number. No one really had a good estimate of how many *khariji* madrasahs there were not affiliated to the Madrasah Board. Many said there were ten times as many private madrasahs as there were state-supported ones. It was widely argued that private madrasahs were popular because they offered food and often board and lodging to their students. As Mohammad Salim, the CPI(M) minister, said, "Children whose families cannot afford a square meal would prefer these madrasahs which provide them food, shelter and some sort of education."[18] The point was made repeatedly that madrasahs were never the first choice considered by Muslim parents, at least for their sons. They would always prefer the regular secondary school if they could afford it. The religious professions did not have much attraction for most young Muslims who went into them only because the alternative was low-paid and unskilled manual work. Even those who spoke so loudly about the right of minorities to run their own schools did not send their own children to madrasahs. Private madrasahs were coming up because there was a social need that the state had been unable to fill; the community was stepping in where the government had failed.

How did the private madrasahs raise their funds? Community leaders insisted that charity was a religious duty for Muslims, and many took that obligation seriously. Most private madrasahs ran on money and food collected from families in the neighborhood. Yes, there were also a few large Islamic foundations, even some that received funds from international foundations based in Saudi Arabia and the Gulf states, and these sometimes made grants to private madrasahs. A few private madrasahs in West Bengal possessed large buildings and provided free boarding to three or four hundred students each; such resources could not have been raised locally. But the administrators of these madrasahs resented the suggestion that this was tainted money. All grants, they insisted, were legal and had to be cleared by the relevant ministries in Delhi.[19]

What about the content of the courses taught at these private madrasahs? There were some sensational stories in the mainstream press that quoted from some of the primers that allegedly glorified *jihadi* warriors and demanded that the civil code be replaced by the *sharia*.[20] But once again, it was clear that most Muslim representatives, irrespective of political loyalties, had a low opinion of the quality of education offered by the private madrasahs. Their complaint was that the state-supported schools were few and not necessarily better run, and alternative secular private education was too expensive.

The West Bengal debate brought forward an important fact that seems to me crucial in judging the conditions for a democratic politics of secularism. The issue could not be successfully posed as one of a secularizing state versus a minority community seeking to preserve its cultural identity. Although the tendency was powerful, it did not win the day. There were several interventions that made the point that the question of social reform was one that was emerging *from within* the Muslim community itself. The latter tendency too was by no means decisive, but it was there. Not only that, it was strongly influencing the question of who represents the minority community. The issues were well brought out in an article by Mainul Hasan, a CPI(M) member of parliament from Murshidabad.[21]

After going through the history of madrasah education and the recent changes in curricula, Mainul Hasan disputes the argument that private madrasahs were growing because there were not enough secondary schools. Speaking as an insider, he argues that a major reason for the initiative within the community to start madrasahs was to provide jobs to Muslim young men. Most madrasahs were set up as a result of local community initiative, often with the support of political parties. It was possible to raise funds from within the community through charitable donations (*zaqat, fitra,* etc.). Most madrasahs ran on shoestring budgets. But they provided employment to educated Muslims who would teach in private madrasahs, become maulvis in mosques and lecture round the year at religious congregations. These were necessary, even if not very lucrative, functions, and Muslims with a smattering of education had few other opportunities open to them.

The rest of the article is a strong plea for further modernization of madrasahs. No Muslim could claim that modern education was not necessary. On the other hand, everyone was agreed that private madrasahs did not provide modern education. Why then should not the government come forward to start modern madrasahs that were not "factories for producing mullahs"? The Muslim community should not only support this policy but also actively contribute, even financially, to the setting up of madrasahs that offer modern education.

Finally, the question of subversive propaganda and terrorism. Mainul Hasan takes the clear position that administering the law and protecting the security of the country is the government's responsibility. It was childish, he says, to claim that the community and not the police would act against organizations that were involved in subversive activities. Rather, the duty of the community was to provide the necessary context within which the government could make correct policies and implement them properly. Suppose, he says, an imam of a mosque is liked and respected by the community; he has been leading the prayers for many years. It then turns out that he is actually from Bangladesh and does not have the right papers to live and work in this country. No one can dispute the fact that his status is illegal. But it may be that the correct policy would be to persuade the authorities to help him get the right papers. This the community must try to do, but it cannot insist that the state should not act when there is a violation of the law.

IV

Who represents the minorities? The question was raised directly in the debate over madrasahs. After the chief minister's meeting with Muslim intellectuals and madrasah teachers, complaints were heard in party circles over the ceremonial recitation from the Quran at the meeting.[22] Why should a meeting with representatives of the Muslim community inevitably mean a meeting with imams and maulanas? The answer clearly was that there were few organized forums in the public sphere outside the religious institutions that could claim to be representative of a community that was marked as a *religious* minority. Why was that the case in West Bengal where a fifth of the population is Muslim and where there is a growing Muslim middle class? Because, as several Muslim professionals explained, community organizations tended to be dominated by men from the religious occupations who were suspicious and resentful of those Muslims who had successfully made it into the urban secular professions. The overwhelming majority of Muslims in West Bengal were rural and poor; urban middle-class Muslims were not able, and perhaps did not wish, to represent them. As one Muslim bureaucrat remarked, "The uneducated or semi-educated lot is intolerant, fanatical and dangerous."

It was not uncommon for professional Muslims with liberal opinions to be targeted for vilification by communal organizations. As a result, such persons usually chose to stay away from community organizations altogether, leaving them to the unchallenged sway of men flaunting their religious credentials. As one correspondent writing to a leading Bengali daily put it, almost twenty percent of all students in regular secondary schools in West Bengal are Muslims. Yet it is the private madrasah question, involving only a few thousand students, that agitates the political circle. "How much longer will political leaders succumb to the imams and put a lid on reforms within Muslim society?" she asked. Muslim politicians in state and national politics were invariably educated in mainstream institutions and were often in the secular professions. Yet every time there is a debate over reform in Muslim society, it is the imams who are listened to as representatives of the community. "The principal obstacle," she claimed, "in the fight against Muslim fundamentalism and religious bigotry is the silence of the growing educated and enlightened section of Muslim society."[23]

The question then arises: what are the appropriate institutions through which the debate over change within minority communities can be conducted in a secular polity? Ever since independence, while the modernizing state in India has often sought to change traditional social institutions and practices by legal and administrative intervention, an accompanying demand has always been that the minority religious communities must have the right to protect their religious and cultural identities, because otherwise they would be at the mercy of a majoritarian politics of homogenization. The Indian state, in general, has largely stayed away from pushing an interventionist agenda of modernization with respect to the institutions and practices of minority communities. This, in turn, has produced a vicious campaign in recent years from the Hindu right wing accusing the Indian state and the parties of the center and the left of "pseudo-secularism and appeasement of minorities." Even in the case of West Bengal, as we saw, the suggestion that private madrasahs might come under government regulation provoked enough of an outcry from those who claimed to represent the Muslim community to force the government to make what many saw as a climb-down. The alternative, to work for reform from within the community institutions, is seen by most potential reformers as too difficult and infeasible. Once again, even in the case of West Bengal, we have seen that factors of class, occupation, and ideological orientation stand in the way of liberal middle-class Muslims from engaging in community institutions.

There is, however, a third possibility which, it seems to me, is visible even within the context of the recent West Bengal debate. It is not a dominant tendency, but it has become a distinct presence. This reformist intervention takes place not exclusively within the legal-administrative apparatus of the state. Nor does it take place in the nonpolitical zone of civil society. Rather, it works in that overlap between the extensive governmental functions of development and welfare and the workings of community institutions that I have elsewhere called *political society*. This is often a zone of paralegal practices, opposed to the civic norms of proper citizenship. Yet there are attempts here to devise new, and often contextual and transitory, norms of fairness and justice in making available the welfare and developmental functions of government to large sections of poor and underprivileged people. There are claims of representation here that have to be established on that overlapping zone between the governmental functions and the community institutions. I see in the West Bengal case an attempt to pursue a campaign of reform through the agency of *political* representatives rather than either through state intervention or through civil social action. Those political representatives of the Left parties in West Bengal who are Muslims usually have large popular support among their Muslim constituents because of their promise, if not ability, to deliver benefits such as jobs, health, education, water, roads, electricity, etc. But as political representatives of the minority community, they do not necessarily relinquish their right to speak on the internal affairs of the community, if only because the community institutions are also tied into the network of governmental functions. As Mainul Hasan pointed out, even the private madrasahs had to be set up with the active involvement of local political leaders. This is the zone where a different mode of reformist intervention can take place that straddles government and community, outside and inside. It can potentially democratize the question of who represents the minorities.

I have presented here only the hint of a different modality of secular politics. I am stressing its significance as a potential, but I must not exaggerate its actuality. As a student of Hindu-Muslim re-

lations in Bengal in the twentieth century, I have lived far too closely
with the massive evidence of communal violence there to have rosy
ideas about any sort of innate secularism of the Bengali people,
whether Hindu or Muslim. Indeed, I often worry about the compla-
cency of many left and liberal persons who think that the communal
question has been somehow resolved in West Bengal and Bangladesh.
On the other hand, I do think that there is a deeply democratic im-
plication of the massive political mobilization that has taken place in
rural West Bengal in the last three decades. It is well known that
democracy itself is no guarantee of secularism, since electoral majorities can often be mobilized against minority communities: we see
this only too well in Gujarat today. On the other hand, it is also true
that protected minority rights give a premium to traditionalists and
even fundamentalists within the minority communities unless the
question of who represents them is allowed to be negotiated within
a more effective democratic process. I see something of this process
going on in West Bengal's political society.

But the other point that has been also emphasized in this controversy is the limit set by the parameters of global politics on political
possibilities inherent in the local situation. The trends in global politics initiated by the United States following the events of September
11, 2001 have put new constraints on political society in most of the
world. The imperial privileges that are now being asserted in carrying
out the so-called "war on terror," the arrogant disregard for established international laws and procedures, the abrogation of the civic
rights of both citizens and foreign residents in the name of homeland
security and, above all, the global spread of the ubiquitous and infinitely malleable concepts of "the terrorist" and "those that sympathize
with terrorism"—labels that can be attached to almost any individuals, groups, ethnicities, or nationalities whose political desires happen to draw the ire of ruling regimes and dominant powers—can
have only a negative impact on popular politics. As I have frequently
pointed out, political society is not like a gentleman's club; it can
often be a nasty and dangerous place. When violent and hateful mobilizations in political society can draw their legitimacy from the cyn-

ical deployment of state violence by those who claim to speak for the free societies of modernity, the less glamorous projects of patient, humane, and democratic social transformation are liable to come under severe strain. One only hopes that while it is the former that is making most of the news today, history is being made through the latter endeavors.

SEVEN

Are Indian Cities Becoming Bourgeois At Last?

Or, if you prefer, we could exclaim: Are Indian cities becoming bourgeois, alas?

I

No matter what the underlying sentiment, there are several reasons for asking a question such as this. First, it is evident that there has been in the last decade or so a concerted attempt to clean up the Indian cities, to rid streets and public lands of squatters and encroachers, and to reclaim public spaces for the use of proper citizens. This movement has been propelled by citizens' groups and staunchly supported by an activist judiciary claiming to defend the rights of citizens to a healthy environment in which everyone abides by the law. Second, while there continues in every Indian metropolis a process of the suburbanization of the middle class, there has been at the same time a growing concern, expressed in the form of organized movements and legal regulations, for the preservation of the architectural and cultural heritage of the historic city, whether precolonial or colonial. Third, even as public spaces are reclaimed for the general use of proper citizens, there is a proliferation of segre-

Delivered at the plenary session of the City One Conference organized by Sarai at the Centre for the Study of Developing Societies, Delhi, on January 11–13, 2003.

gated and protected spaces for elite consumption, elite lifestyles, and elite culture.

This is in many ways a reversal of the pattern established by the post-independence Indian city. That pattern was one in which—in the 1950s and 1960s—the urban elite produced in the days of colonial rule exercised their social and political dominance over the city, replacing the Europeans in positions of governmental authority and working out methods of control over the new institutions of mass electoral representation. In Calcutta, for instance, wealthy landlords and professionals became the patrons, and often the elected representatives, of the ruling Congress party. The wealthy were at the forefront of a general middle-class involvement in providing social, cultural, and moral leadership to the urban neighborhood. There was usually a quite dense network of neighborhood institutions such as schools, sports clubs, markets, tea shops, libraries, parks, religious gatherings, charitable organizations, and so on, organized and supported by the wealthy and the middle classes, through which an active and participatory sense of urban community was created and nurtured. It was then normal rather than exceptional for middle-class children to go to the neighborhood school and play in the neighborhood park; for young men to assemble for *adda* in the neighborhood club or tea shop; for housewives to take out books from the neighborhood library or buy clothes at the neighborhood market; for the elderly to converge on a neighborhood institution to listen to religious discourses and devotional music. Most neighborhoods were mixed in terms of class. A street front lined by large mansions or elegant middle-class houses would invariably hide crowded slums at the back where the service population would live. The industrial areas of the city, of course, contained huge slum-dwelling populations. The urban poor were, however, frequently tied to the wealthy in patron-client relationships that were not merely personal but often mediated by charitable organizations and even proto-unions, as Dipesh Chakrabarty showed in his book on the jute workers of Calcutta.[1] Even when the industrial working class was organized by political activists, the unions provided an active link between the middle-class intelligentsia and the slum-dwelling workers.

At least as far as the city of Calcutta is concerned, I would argue that the social and political dominance of the wealthy and the cultural leadership of the middle class were sustained in the first two decades after independence through a grid of neighborhood institutions that attempted to create and nurture neighborhood communities. Calcutta neighborhoods were not homogeneous by class, and they were frequently mixed in terms of language, religion, or ethnicity.[2] While social boundaries between the classes were clearly maintained in different contexts, the sense of community cutting across classes was also actively fostered through the idea of the neighborhood or *para*. Apart from the daily support provided to this idea by the neighborhood institutions, there were also periodic congregations of large numbers of residents on occasions such as a football match between the local team and a team from another *para*, or the open-air theater and music performances in the local park, or the annual Durga Puja. However, these community formations, mixed in terms of class, were, for the most part, homogeneous in terms of language, religion, or ethnicity. Nirmal Kumar Bose, who studied this phenomenon closely in the early 1960s, found that in their social ties, if not always in their residential choices, ethnic groups in Calcutta tended to cluster together. Each ethnic community, defined by religion or language, although overlapping with others across the space of the neighborhoods, was in effect separate. Not only Bengalis, but Marwaris, Oriyas, Urdu-speaking Muslims, Anglo-Indians, Gujaratis, Punjabis, Chinese—each had their own network of associations. Bose's somewhat disheartening conclusion was that "the diverse ethnic groups in the population of the city have come to bear the same relation to one another as do the castes in India as a whole."[3] In fact, given the proportion of Bengali speakers in the city—about 63 percent in 1961—and the fact that the only ethnically homogeneous neighborhoods were the ones peopled by Bengali speakers, the position of Bengalis in the city of Calcutta could be said to have been somewhat similar to that of the dominant caste in many regions of rural India. The density and visibility of public life in the Bengali neighborhoods produced the appearance of the city itself as a predominantly Bengali city.

But a caste-like associational life sustained by patron-client relationships with the wealthy and the powerful is not exactly compatible with the definition of bourgeois public life in a modern city. Clearly Calcutta, like other Indian cities in the 1950s and 1960s, had failed to make the transition to proper urban modernity. Nirmal Bose, in a famous article in the *Scientific American* in 1965, called Calcutta a "premature metropolis ... out of phase with history ... having appeared in the setting of the traditional agricultural economy in advance of the industrial revolution that is supposed to beget the metropolis."[4] Dipesh Chakrabarty's conclusion about the nature of working-class organization and consciousness in industrial Calcutta was no different: the persistence of pre-bourgeois modes of sociality in factories and slums, he argued, impaired the ability of workers to act as a class.[5] I remember after my first visit to Bombay in the early 1970s feeling envious of what I took to be a wonderfully modern and organic relationship between that city and its bourgeoisie. Greater familiarity with the history of Bombay soon disabused me of the idea. If Calcutta was not modern and bourgeois, neither was Bombay. The discovery was comforting.

II

The old structure of social-political dominance was largely transformed in the 1970s and 1980s by the twin effects of democracy and development. On the one hand, rival political parties intensified their efforts to mobilize electoral support in the cities. On the other hand, the huge increase in the population of the big cities, caused mainly by migrations from the countryside, created explosive social conditions marked by political unrest, crime, homelessness, squalor, and disease. This led to a new concern for providing housing, sanitation, water, electricity, transport, schools, health services, etc. aimed specially at the urban poor. In these decades, there was a proliferation of developmental and welfare schemes, mostly with central government funding and often with substantial international aid from agencies such as the World Bank, for accommodating the burgeoning population of the poor within the structures of urban life, even as those structures were being pressed to their limits.

The demands of electoral mobilization, on the one hand, and the logic of welfare distribution, on the other, overlapped and came together. I have elsewhere described this terrain as *political society*, to distinguish it from the classical notion of civil society. Governmental administration of welfare for the urban poor necessarily had to follow a different logic from that of the normal relations of the state with citizens organized in civil society. The city poor frequently lived as squatters on public land, traveled on public transport without paying, stole water and electricity, encroached on streets and parks. Given the available resources, it was unrealistic to insist that they first mend their ways and turn into proper citizens before they become eligible for governmental benefits. The various urban development projects of the 1970s and 1980s took it for granted that large sections of the poor would have to live in the city without legitimate title to their places of habitation. The authorities nevertheless provided slums with water and sanitation, schools, and health centers. Electricity companies negotiated collective rates with entire squatter settlements in order to cut down the losses from pilferage. Suburban railway authorities in Bombay and Calcutta, when calculating their budgets, routinely assumed that half or more of daily commuters would not buy tickets. Populations of the urban poor had to be pacified and even cared for, partly because they provided the necessary labor and services to the city's economy and partly because if they were not cared for at all, they could endanger the safety and well-being of all citizens.

The general attitude of the times was represented almost emblematically in the widespread revulsion around the country when the news spread of the forcible demolition of slums and eviction of residents from the Turkman Gate area of Delhi during the period of the Emergency. Sanjay Gandhi's zealousness in cleaning up the city was seen as antithetical to the democratic culture of the postcolonial city. The attitude was also reflected in the general willingness of the judiciary in the 1980s to come to the aid of the urban poor, virtually recognizing that they had a right to a habitation and a livelihood in the city and that government authorities could not evict or penalize them at will without providing for some sort of resettlement and rehabilitation.

It would be wrong, however, to think that this process represented an extension of citizenship to the poor. It did not. In fact, as I have argued at greater length elsewhere, a careful conceptual distinction was made between citizens and populations. Populations are empirical categories of people with specific social or economic attributes that are relevant for the administration of developmental or welfare policies. Thus, there may be specific schemes for slum-dwelling children or working mothers below the poverty line, or, say, for settlements prone to flooding in the rainy season. Each scheme of this type, or the broader policy within which it is formulated, will identify distinct population groups whose size and specific socioeconomic or cultural characteristics will be empirically determined and recorded through censuses and surveys. Populations then are produced by the classificatory schemes of governmental knowledge. Unlike citizenship, which carries the moral connotation of sharing in the sovereignty of the state and hence of claiming rights in relation to the state, populations do not bear any inherent moral claim. When they are looked after by governmental agencies, they merely get the favor of a policy whose rationale is one of costs and benefits in terms of economic, political, or social outcomes. When these calculations change, the policies change too and so does the composition of the target groups. In fact, if I could make a general theoretical point here without elaborating on my reasons, I would say that the governmental administration of development and welfare produced a heterogeneous social, consisting of multiple population groups to be addressed through multiple and flexible policies. This was in sharp contrast with the conception of citizenship in which the insistence on the homogeneous national was both fundamental and relentless.

There were obvious reasons why population groups belonging to the urban poor could not be treated on a par with proper citizens. If squatters were to be given any kind of legitimacy by government authorities in their illegal occupation of public or private lands, then the entire structure of legally held property would be threatened. Large sections of the urban poor could not be treated as legitimate citizens precisely because their habitation and livelihood were so often premised on a violation of the law. And yet, as I have mentioned before, there were powerful social and political reasons for extending certain kinds of benefits and protection to these populations as necessary inhabitants of the city. Officials from diverse agencies such as the municipal authorities, the police, the health services, transport departments, electric supply companies, etc. devised numerous ways in which such facilities and benefits could be extended on a case-to-case, *ad hoc,* or exceptional basis, without jeopardizing the overall structure of legality and property. One might say that this was perhaps the most remarkable development in the governance of Indian cities in the 1970s and 1980s—the emergence of an entire substructure of paralegal arrangements, created or at least recognized by the governmental authorities, for the integration of low-wage laboring and service populations into the public life of the city.

These arrangements were not, and indeed could not be, worked out on the terrain of relations between civil society and the state. That was a terrain inhabited by proper citizens whose relations with the state were framed within a structure of constitutionally protected rights. Associations of citizens in civil society could demand the attention of governmental authorities as a matter of right, because they represented citizens who observed the law. The authorities could not treat associations of squatters or pavement hawkers on the same footing as legitimate associations of civil society.

The relations of government agencies with population groups of the urban poor were determined not on the terrain of civil society but on that of political society. This was the terrain of the heterogeneous social, where multiple and flexible policies were put into operation, producing multiple and strategic responses from population groups seeking to adapt to, cope with, or make use of these policies. Policies on this terrain of governmentality are never simply a matter of disbursing charity. Rather, there is always an attempt to calibrate rewards and costs, incentives and punishments, in order to produce the desired outcomes. Thus, slums may be provided with sanitation in the expectation that slum-dwellers would not dirty the streets or parks. If this does not work out as expected, a different structure of rewards and costs might be tried. Clearly, this creates a field of continuous negotiation between the authorities and the population group. What benefits would be given to which groups and for how long depend on a series of strategic negotiations.

This is the field of political society. We are not talking here of relations between the state and citizens in civil society. On the contrary, these are relations between population groups and governmental agencies administering policy. To play the game of strategic political negotiations with the authorities, population groups too must organize themselves. Governmental policy will always seek to deal with them as discrete elements of the heterogeneous social. It is the task of political organization to mold the empirical discreteness of a population group into the moral solidarity of a community. This is what was frequently achieved in urban political society in India in the 1970s and 1980s.

It involved opening up a field of mobilization and mediation by political leaders and parties. The old structure of patron-client relations between the wealthy elite and the middle classes on the one side and the poor on the other was rapidly transformed. The politics of governmental administration of welfare schemes for the poor produced an entirely new field of competitive mobilization by political parties and leaders. One of the most significant processes that took place in this period in old industrial cities like Bombay and Calcutta was the decline in the effectiveness of trade unions organized around the factory and the rise of organized movements centered on the slum. In Bombay, the communist-led trade unions were crushed, first, by the movements led by the maverick labor organizer Datta Samant, and then through the organized network of neighborhood-based branches of the Hindu-chauvinist right-wing Shiv Sena. In Calcutta, there was first an assault of state terror in 1971–72 on activists of the CPI(M-L) and the CPI(M) in which more than a thousand were killed and several thousand put in prison or driven away from their homes. Until the end of the Emergency in 1977, there was virtually no political activity of the communist parties allowed in the city. It was in this period that the younger leaders of the Congress Party of Indira Gandhi put in place the structure of the new urban political society. Once again, it was based primarily on the neighborhood, often meticulously demarcated to identify as clearly as possible who belonged to which local association. These local groupings then sought representation by the political leader or party in order both to protect themselves from punitive action by the authorities and to seek the benefits of governmental policy. When the communists returned to the city's politics after 1977, they too proceeded to organize the neighborhoods along the same lines. Interestingly, even though the Left parties have now ruled in West Bengal for more than twenty-five years, many of the structures of support built by the Congress leaders in the older sections of Calcutta in the early 1970s have remained intact.

Competitive electoral mobilization of the poor in the 1970s and 1980s afforded them a new strategic resource. They could now exercise, or at least threaten to exercise, a choice. If one leader or party could not get things done for them, they could threaten to switch sides and vote for the rival party in the next election. This, in fact, has happened on numerous occasions in the big Indian cities. Of course, since a great deal of these negotiations in political society involves activities that violate the law, there is always more than a hint of violence in them. Often, effective mobilization in political society means the controlled organization of violence, precisely because the security of the peaceful legality of civil society is not always available here. One can produce numerous examples of this from the *chawls* and *juggis* of Bombay, Delhi, Calcutta or Madras. The recent book by Thomas Blom Hansen on the Shiv Sena in Bombay contains the most systematic study I know of this phenomenon.[6]

III

The situation has now changed once more. Since the 1990s, and perhaps most dramatically in the last five years or so, there has been an apparent shift in the ruling attitudes toward the big city in India. This is what prompted my initial question in this talk: Are Indian cities becoming bourgeois at last? It is not that there has been a retreat of political society as it existed in the 1980s. It may simply be that along with a change in governmental policies toward the city, the particular population groups organized under political society have changed. But there has been without doubt a surge in the activities and visibility of civil society. In metropolis after Indian metropolis, organized civic groups have come forward to demand from the administration and the judiciary that laws and regulations for the proper use of land, public spaces, and thoroughfares be formulated and strictly adhered to in order to improve the quality of life of citizens. Everywhere the dominant cry seems to be to rid the city of encroachers and polluters and, as it were, to give the city back to its proper citizens.

To understand the reasons for this change, I believe it is necessary to consider the place of the city in the modern Indian imagination. It has often been pointed out that unlike the numerous innovative and passionately ideological projects to either preserve or transform rural India, the period of nationalism produced little fundamental thinking about the desired Indian city of the future. Gyan Prakash has recently considered this question.[7] The paradox is indeed very curious, because the place of colonial modernity in India in the nineteenth and twentieth centuries was obviously the city and that is where India's nationalist elite was produced. Yet, two or three generations of social and political thinkers, scholars and artists, poets and novelists, living and working in the era of nationalism, devoted most of their imaginative energies to the task of producing an idea not of the future Indian city but of a rural India fit for the modern age.

The answer to the paradox perhaps lies in a perceived lack of agency by the Indian elite in thinking about the city. The industrial city, like modern industry itself, was unquestionably a creation of Western modernity. The colonial cities of British India were largely creations of British colonial rulers to which Indians had adapted. There was, it seems to me, always a sense among the middle classes of the great colonial cities of India of not being in control of their surroundings. Ramakrishna Paramahamsa, who wielded considerable spiritual influence over the Calcutta middle class at the end of the nineteenth century, often told his devotees about the housemaid who spent a whole lifetime living and working in a rich household in the city. She would call her employer's house her home, but in her heart of hearts she knew that that was not her home; her home was far away in the village.[8] For a long time, perhaps not until the 1950s, the metropolis had not acquired in the minds of the Indian middle class the moral security and stability of home.

Even when it became an irrevocable fact that their lives and futures were necessarily tied to the fate of the city, the middle classes were deeply ambivalent. Something of the popular attitude toward the big city as a deeply profane place, corrupted by money and commerce and littered with dangerously seductive amusements, was shared by the urban middle classes as well. This can be seen from as early a period as the 1820s when Bhabanicharan Bandyopadhyay wrote *Kalikata kamalalay*, possibly the first text of urban sociology in India.[9] In time, as the extended family crumbled under the pressures of economic change, a new ethic of the nuclear family was sought for. But this new ethic regarded the external world of the city—its schools, streets, parks, markets, theatres—as dangerous for the family and especially for children growing up in an urban environment.[10] The middle class proceeded to exercise its moral influence over these urban institutions, building in the process the structures of the moral community of the neighborhood that I earlier described for Calcutta in the 1950s and 1960s.

But there was still something that was apparently beyond control. What was the imagined morphology—the moral map, if you will— of the Indian industrial metropolis? The Western models had been copied under the aegis of the colonial rulers, with mixed results. When the models failed to deliver the predicted outcomes, urban Indians simply adapted themselves to the imperfect copies of the original, often producing reactions like Nirmal Bose's lament about the "premature metropolis." But there were no new models of the Indian industrial metropolis. When Jawaharlal Nehru invited Le Corbusier to build Chandigarh, a city of the future untrammeled by Indian history and tradition, it was probably not so much a utopian dream as a sign of desperation, because no organic idea of the Indian city of the future was available to him.

As the Indian metropolis exploded in the 1970s, the attempt was made, as I have said before, to contain the impact and pacify the threatened consequences through welfare policies aimed particularly at the urban poor. It meant putting up with numerous violations of civic norms and regulations for the sake of accommodating population groups that did not have adequate resources to afford a decent life in the city. Urban services were often strained to the point of collapse and the quality of the urban environment deteriorated rapidly. For the most part, the overcrowding and squalor were accepted as inevitable elements of third world industrialization. It was unfair, the argument went, to expect the same quality of life as in Western cities. Wasn't the same thing happening in other cities of the third world—in Mexico City, São Paulo, Lagos, Cairo, Bangkok, Manila, etc. etc.?

The management of the urban poor on the terrain of political society in the 1970s and 1980s meant, among other things, not only the passing of the old dominance of the wealthy over the politics of the city but also, more significantly, a disengagement of the middle classes from the hurly burly of urban politics. This, it seems to me, was an important precondition for the transformation of the 1990s. While the messy business of striking deals between municipal authorities, the police, property developers, criminal gangs, slum dwellers, or pavement hawkers was left to the unsavory class of local politicians, proper citizens retreated into civil society. Middle-class activism, even when it engaged with the lives of the urban poor, as it often did, was deliberately restricted to the strictly nonpolitical world of the NGOs.

In the 1990s a new idea of the post-industrial city became globally available for emulation. This is the city that has seen the demise of traditional manufacturing that was the engine of the industrial revolution. The new city is driven not by manufacturing but by finance and a host of producer services. As national economies around the world become integrated with the globalized network of capital and as manufacturing and even services are dispersed from the old industrial cities of Europe and North America to locations all over the world, the need for centralization of managerial control becomes greater. The new city is characterized by a central business district with advanced transport and telecommunication facilities and office space. This is the node of an inter-metropolitan and global network carrying out information processing and control functions. Apart from management and financial operations, certain kinds of services, such as advertising, accounting, legal services, banking, tend to be centralized in the business district.

The new organization of business firms creates a demand for a large range of service inputs bought in the market rather than produced in-house. The growth of the new metropolis is fundamentally characterized by a shift from industrial manufacturing to a service-dominated urban economy. Outside the central business district, therefore, the rest of the city is characterized by an urban space that is increasingly differentiated in social terms, even as it is functionally interconnected beyond the physical contiguity of neighborhoods. Thus, there are new segregated and exclusive spaces for the managerial and technocratic elite. These could be in exclusive suburbs as in several American cities or in renewed and refurbished sections of the historic city as in Paris, Amsterdam, Brussels, Rome, or Milan. The new high-technology industries tend to be located in the newest and most environmentally attractive peripheries of the metropolis. At the same time, while the new metropolis is globally connected, it is frequently locally disconnected from large sections of its population who are functionally unnecessary and are often seen to be socially or politically disruptive.[11]

This idea of the new post-industrial globalized metropolis began to circulate in India sometime in the 1990s. Bangalore was the city that was said to be the most likely to fit the bill, but Hyderabad soon announced its claim too. I suspect, however, that the idea of what a city should be and look like has now been deeply influenced by this post-industrial global image everywhere among the urban middle classes in India. The atmosphere produced by economic liberalization has had something to do with it. Far more influential has been the intensified circulation of images of global cities through cinema, television, and the internet as well as through the Indian middle classes' far greater access to international travel. Government policy, at the level of the states and even the municipalities, has been directly affected by the urgent pressure to connect with the global economy and attract foreign investment. The result has been, on the one hand, greater assertion by organizations of middle-class citizens of their right to unhindered access to public spaces and thoroughfares and to a clean and healthy urban environment. On the other hand, government policy has rapidly turned away from the idea of helping the poor to subsist within the city and is instead paying the greatest attention to improving infrastructure in order to create conditions for the import of high technology and the new service industries. Thus, manufacturing industries are being moved out beyond the city limits; squatters and encroachers are being evicted; property and tenancy laws are being rewritten to enable market forces to rapidly convert the congested and dilapidated sections of the old city into high-value commercial and residential districts. If this is the new global bourgeois vision of twenty-first century urbanity, then this time we may have successfully grasped it.

However, the expected social and political costs have probably not yet been estimated. There is little doubt that the new metropolis will be a place of new social disparities. Unlike the middle class produced by state-led industrialization and import substitution, the new metropolitan economy is unlikely to produce an expanding middle class. Rather, it will depend on exports to the international market and consumption of services by organizations rather than individuals. The new metropolis will belong to the managerial and technocratic elite and a new class of very highly paid workers—professionals, middle and lower-level managers, brokers, and middlemen of all kinds. The elite will form its own community—a spatially bound, interpersonally networked subculture built around the business center, segregated residential areas, exclusive restaurants, country clubs, arts and culture complexes, and easy access to airports. While it may concede the general administration of the city to democratically elected representatives, the managerial elite will probably resist any interference by the political leadership in strategic decisionmaking that affects business prospects. The new consumer industries will be driven not, as in the old days, by the market created by thrifty middle-class families, but by the new high-spending workers. This is where a new, globally urban, consumer lifestyle and aesthetic will take root. There will be segregated and exclusive spaces for shops, restaurants, arts, and entertainment aimed at this clientele. The new economy will also need its share of low-wage workers. They will probably commute long distances because, without the protection of the old developmental state, they could hardly afford to live in the city. Large sections of the older inhabitants of the city will, however, become unnecessary to the new economy. Will they accept their redundancy without protest? Will they react to the new and glaring social disparities? If democracy has indeed taken root in India's cities, will political society provide the instruments for negotiating a controlled transition to a new urban regime or will it explode into anarchic resistance?

These are the great unresolved questions that confront our urban present. Perhaps there will be no catastrophe. As Ashis Nandy has reassured us so often, like science, cricket, cinema, medicine, and even terrorism, this time too our native vernacular genius will corrupt the imported model of the post-industrial city and turn it into an impure, inefficient, but ultimately less malevolent hybrid. I must confess, however, that the evidence so far is not very comforting. In the city of Calcutta, located in a state that has seen in its rural areas some of the most positive results of the operation of political society, historical conditions have ensured the painful death of traditional urban industry. This, combined with the new market forces, has caused a steady decline in absolute population over the last two decades in more than half of the wards of the northern and central parts of the city. Thus, there has been a growing suburbanization of the Bengali middle class—so much so that in the Calcutta metropolitan district as a whole, Bengali speakers are now only 51 percent of the population, while within the old municipal area they probably number no more than 40 percent (compared to 63 percent in 1961). Even more striking is the fact that whereas 22 percent of the city's population are migrants from other states of India, only 12 percent are from other parts of West Bengal. Clearly, unlike in the 1960s and 1970s, the demand for low-wage labor in the city is no longer supplied by rural migrants from Calcutta's hinterland. This is corroborated by another striking fact: as much as one-fifth of the city's Bengali-speakers, both men and women, are university graduates.[12] This is a tribute to the success of land reforms and agricultural development in rural West Bengal that has stopped the impoverishment of small peasants and provided work throughout the year in the countryside to the landless. But it has had the unintended, and profoundly ironic, consequence of threatening the cultural leadership of the Bengali middle class over its beloved city.

The response, as far as I can see it, is thoroughly confused, almost mindless. On the one hand, after tripping over numerous ideological hurdles, the political leadership has been finally cornered into acknowledging that the economic revival of Calcutta depends on high technology industry, supported by foreign investment and producing for the global market. To create conditions for this, the city must be refurbished and new infrastructure put in place. All of the processes I have described of reconstituting the urban space to fit the model of the post-industrial city have been initiated in Calcutta with government sponsorship, including eviction of squatters and pavement stalls, clearing of slums to make way for office blocks and apartment buildings, exclusive shopping malls, segregated and rigorously policed residential areas for the affluent, etc. If there is a plan behind these policies, and if that plan is to succeed, what we should get is a metropolis integrated into the circuits of global capital, culturally dominated by the new managers, technocrats, professionals, and middlemen belonging to, or at least aspiring to belong to, a globalized cosmopolitan subculture. Yet, the other response of the political leadership has been to assert a new Bengali-ness, beginning with changing by law the English and Hindustani names of Calcutta to Kolkata and threatening to enforce several other measures to reinscribe the cultural dominance of the Bengali middle class over a city that it has physically abandoned.

It is possible that the absence of a plan—a moral map or an imagined morphology—is not a bad thing. Perhaps that is how vernacular resistance to global designs ultimately succeeds. And yet, I seriously worry about the capacity of unselfconscious local practice to beat back the formidable challenges posed by the material as well as the imaginative forces of the new regime of globality. May be it is only an occupational disease I suffer from, but I cannot help imagining that gatherings of self-conscious people will provide some clues to thinking through, rather than merely stumbling upon, the path leading to the future of Indian cities. It will make no difference to history if I am wrong. But if I am right, it will be a considerable reward for our collective efforts.

Afterword
The Ides of March

There is a gnawing sense of inevitability in the way things are moving. The flood is rising inch by inch; the only question is when the dike will burst. Except, this is not a natural disaster waiting to happen. These are events fully under the control of world leaders playing for high stakes. Why is the world being pushed to the precipice?

To begin with, let us set aside the high-sounding moral reasons for going to war with Iraq. Not even their proponents believe in them, except as linguistic instruments for pushing a diplomatic point. Not only are these moral reasons applied selectively—Iraq, not North Korea; Iraq, not Saudi Arabia or Pakistan; Iraq, not Israel—thus confirming the charge of double standards; they are also changed to suit the requirements of the diplomatic game. We were first told that the real goal of military action would be to change the regime and liberate Iraq. Then when it became necessary to seek support in the United Nations, the objective was changed to the disarmament of Iraq. Now, when UN support looks unlikely, the moral case is once more the removal of Saddam Hussein and the liberation of Iraq. Who will believe that these moral arguments are anything more than instrumental devices—dressed-up language designed to secure other ends?

What then are the real objectives? There is little doubt that the current chain of events was suddenly set in motion by President Bush

Originally published in *The Telegraph* (Calcutta), March 18, 2003. Reprinted by permission.

in August 2002. We have heard a lot in recent days of the world having waited for twelve long years to see Iraq disarmed. If the UN did indeed fail to act during this time, then surely the United States must share the responsibility for it along with the other key members of the UN. The fact is that there was a general consensus among the world powers that Iraq was being effectively contained. The only dispute was whether the sanctions that the UN had imposed should be lifted. The sudden clamor raised by President Bush over Iraq in August last year took the world diplomatic community by complete surprise.

Why did the U.S. administration decide to turn its sights on Iraq? It is known that sometime in 2002, the most influential group within the administration, consisting of associates of the senior George Bush such as Dick Cheney, Donald Rumsfeld, Paul Wolfowitz, Richard Perle, and others, floated the idea that the situation after the September 11 events had created not so much a crisis as a new opportunity for the United States. The global war against terrorism and the world-wide sympathy for the United States could be turned into a moment for recasting the entire world order and inaugurating "the American century." Instead of containment and deterrence, the United States should assert overwhelming military superiority and the right of pre-emptive strike against any perceived threat. Instead of letting the world's rogue regimes and trouble spots fester under the cloak of national sovereignty, the United States should intervene forcefully to change the political map of the globe and fulfill America's true destiny as benevolent master of a new world empire.

The Middle East was the theatre where this imperial vision could be most dramatically revealed. Get rid of Saddam Hussein and establish a permanent American military presence in Iraq. Try and set up a pliant Iraqi administration, with Iraqi oil revenues paying for the costs. This would put immediate pressure on Saudi Arabia and Syria. The impact would be so huge that the back of the Palestinian *intifada* would be broken. That would be the time to impose a lasting two-state solution on Israel and Palestine. Islamic militancy would lose its most potent rallying cry. Imperial America, driven by a new zeal and purpose, would bring peace to the world.

Moral bigots often acquire a chilling self-confidence that persuades them that all means, no matter how questionable or unpopular, are justified in reaching their ends. The U.S. administration today is led by a right-wing clique whose attitudes and ambitions make it the most reactionary force to have hijacked a Western democracy in recent years. It is known that this group was not in favor of seeking the approval of the United Nations before going to war in Iraq. President Bush was apparently persuaded by Tony Blair and Colin Powell to take the UN route in order to secure greater international legitimacy for military action. Now that the attempt has ended in diplomatic disaster, the UN has become the target of American vilification. Unrestrained abuse is being heaped in the American media, not only on France, but also on an international body that allows countries like Guinea and Angola, full of impoverished and illiterate people, to sit in judgment over American foreign policy. What this reveals about the arrogance and barely concealed racism of American commentators is unsurprising. What is new is the significance of such views for the future of the world order as we have known it.

That is what makes March 2003 such a defining moment. The reason why France, Russia, China, Germany, and so many other members of the Security Council have resisted the so-called second resolution is not because they stand to gain by supporting Saddam Hussein. If anything, they will probably lose a lot by flouting the will of the United States. For one, they will certainly not be invited to the feast of the vultures after the slaughter is over in Iraq. The reason for their resistance is their unwillingness to dismantle the multilateral and democratic world body that was built in the era after decolonization and to put in its place a new structure of imperial hegemony.

What the United States is really demanding is that in the new American century, no country should have the right of veto over the United States. In other words, if the UN is to function as a world body, the United States should be effectively the only country with a veto. The debate over Iraq has thrown the challenge to all nations to decide whether they are prepared to approve that scheme of things. As of now, most have refused. They were in large part emboldened to do so by the unprecedented popular mobilization against the war all round the globe. The United Nations, the world's highest representative body, refused to be coerced into approving a timetable for war unilaterally decided several months ago by American military planners.

The war will now be launched in Iraq without UN approval. Saddam Hussein will be removed and the country will be ravaged. But history will not end there. The American quest for unchallenged hegemony may be consistent with the current distribution of military and economic power in the world. But it is wholly contrary to the democratic spirit of the age. The principles represented by the United Nations belong to democratic institutions everywhere: they are meant to put a check on absolute power. If the UN is to have any meaning, it must be to limit the absolutism of the United States. That battle has not yet been lost. It will be resumed when the costs are tallied of the war and its aftermath. After all, as the now forgotten American commentator Walter Lippmann once reminded his readers, "The consent of the governed is more than a safeguard against ignorant tyrants; it is an insurance against benevolent despots as well."

Notes

NOTES TO CHAPTER 1

1. Benedict Anderson, *Imagined Communities: Reflections on the Origin and Spread of Nationalism* (London: Verso, 1983).

2. Benedict Anderson, *The Spectre of Comparisons: Nationalism, Southeast Asia and the World* (London: Verso, 1998), p. 29.

3. Michel Foucault, "Different Spaces," in James D. Faubion, ed. *Essential Works of Foucault*, vol 2: *Aesthetics, Method, and Epistemology* (New York: New Press, 1998), pp. 175–85.

4. Homi Bhabha, "DissemiNation" in Bhabha, ed., *Nation and Narration* (London: Routledge, 1990), pp. 291–322.

5. "Alumnus, Author of Indian Constitution Honored," *Columbia University Record*, 21, no. 9 (November 3, 1995): 3.

6. B. R. Ambedkar, *Who Were the Shudras? How They Came to be the Fourth Varna in the Indo-Aryan Society* (1946; reprint, Bombay: Thackers, 1970); Ambedkar, *The Untouchables: Who Were They and Why They Became Untouchables* (New Delhi: Amrit Book Company, 1948).

7. Satinath Bhaduri, *Dhorai charitmanas* (vol. 1, 1949; vol. 2, 1951) in *Satinath granthabali*, vol. 2, ed. by Sankha Ghosh and Nirmalya Acharya (Calcutta: Signet, 1973), pp. 1–296.

8. Shahid Amin, "Gandhi as Mahatma" in Ranajit Guha, ed., *Subaltern Studies III* (Delhi: Oxford University Press, 1984), pp. 1–61; Amin, *Event, Metaphor, Memory: Chauri Chaura 1922–1992* (Delhi: Oxford University Press, 1995).

9. M. N. Srinivas, *Social Change in Modern India* (Berkeley: University of California Press, 1966); David Hardiman, *The Coming of the Devi: Adivasi Assertion in Western India* (Delhi: Oxford University Press, 1987).

10. *Dhorai charitmanas*, p. 70.

11. Cited in Gail Omvedt, *Dalits and the Democratic Revolution: Dr. Ambedkar and the Dalit Movement in Colonial India* (New Delhi: Sage, 1994), p. 146.

12. Cited in Omvedt, *Dalits*, pp. 168–9.

13. For accounts of the Poona Pact and the relevant citations, see Ravinder Kumar, "Gandhi, Ambedkar and the Poona Pact, 1932" in Jim Masselos, ed., *Struggling and Ruling: The Indian National Congress, 1885–1985* (New Delhi: Sterling, 1987); Omvedt, *Dalits*, pp. 161–189.

14. Bhabha, "DissemiNation."

15. *Dhorai*, pp. 222–3.

16. B. R. Ambedkar, *Pakistan or the Partition of India* (2nd ed., Bombay: Thacker, 1945).

17. Except by such exemplars of politically sanctioned ignorance and prejudice as Arun Shourie, *Worshipping False Gods: Ambedkar and the Facts Which Have Been Erased* (New Delhi: ASA Publications, 1997).

18. *Pakistan*, p. vii.

19. *Pakistan*, pp. 55–87.

20. *Pakistan*, p. 105.

21. *Pakistan*, pp. 352–58.

22. Anderson, *Spectre*, p. 44.

23. For the story of the legal provision of opportunities for the depressed castes in independent India, see Marc Galanter, *Competing Equalities: Law and the Backward Classes in India* (Delhi: Oxford University Press, 1984).

24. For a recent discussion on Ambedkar's conversion, see Gauri Viswanathan, *Outside the Fold: Conversion, Modernity, and Belief* (Princeton: Princeton University Press, 1998), pp. 211–39.

NOTES TO CHAPTER TWO

1. For instance, in Ibrahim Abu-Lughod, *Arab Rediscovery of Europe: A Study in Cultural Encounters* (Princeton: Princeton University Press, 1963); Timothy Mitchell, *Colonising Egypt* (Cambridge: Cambridge University Press, 1988).

2. Kabir Kausar, *Secret Correspondence of Tipu Sultan* (New Delhi: Light and Life, 1980), pp. 165, 219.

3. James Sutherland, quoted in Sophia Dobson Collet, *The Life and Letters of Raja Rammohun Roy*, ed. Dilip Kumar Biswas and Prabhat Chandra Ganguli (1900; reprint, Calcutta: Sadharan Brahmo Samaj, 1962), p. 308.

4. C. L. R. James, *The Black Jacobins: Toussaint L'Ouverture and the San Domingo Revolution* (New York: Vintage Books, 1963).

5. Cited in Michel-Rolph Trouillot, *Silencing the Past: Power and the Production of History* (Boston: Beacon Press, 1995), p. 79.

6. Trouillot, pp. 70–107.

7. Étienne Balibar, *Masses, Classes, Ideas: Studies on Politics and Philosophy Before and After Marx* (New York: Routledge, 1994).

8. Especially in Karl Marx, "On the Jewish Question" (1843) in Karl Marx and Frederick Engels, *Collected Works*, vol. 3 (Moscow: Progress Publishers, 1975), pp. 146–74.

9. Chapters on "The So-called Primitive Accumulation" in Karl Marx, *Capital*, vol. 1, tr. Samuel Moore and Edward Aveling (Moscow: Progress Publishers, 1954), pp. 667–724.

10. Karl Marx, "The British Rule in India," in Marx and Engels, *Collected Works*, vol. 12, pp. 125–33.

11. Correspondence with Vera Zasulich, in Teodor Shanin, *Late Marx and the Russian Road: Marx and 'the Peripheries of Capitalism'* (London: Routledge and Kegan Paul, 1983); Karl Marx, *The Ethnological Notebooks*, ed. by Lawrence Krader (Assen: Van Gorcum, 1974).

12. Two convenient collections that give a fair sampling of these arguments are Michael Sandel, ed., *Liberalism and Its Critics* (New York: New York University Press, 1984) and Shlomo Avineri and Avner de-Shalit, eds., *Communitarianism and Individualism* (Oxford: Oxford University Press, 1992).

13. See especially Quentin Skinner, *Liberty Before Liberalism* (Cambridge: Cambridge University Press, 1997) and Philip Pettit, *Republicanism: A Theory of Freedom and Government* (Oxford: Oxford University Press, 1997).

14. Pettit, *Republicanism*, p. 241.

15. See, in particular, Michel Foucault, "Governmentality" in Graham Burchell, Colin Gordon and Peter Miller, eds., *The Foucault Effect: Studies in Governmentality* (Chicago: University of Chicago Press, 1991), pp. 87–104.

16. Ian Hacking, *The Taming of Chance* (Cambridge: Cambridge University Press, 1990); Mary Poovey, *Making a Social Body* (Chicago: University of Chicago Press, 1995) and *A History of the Modern Fact* (Chicago: University of Chicago Press, 1998).

17. See in particular Nikolas Rose, *Powers of Freedom: Reframing Political Thought* (Cambridge: Cambridge University Press, 1999); Peter

Miller and Nikolas Rose, "Production, Identity and Democracy," *Theory and Society*, 24 (1995), pp. 427–67; Thomas Osborne, *Aspects of Enlightenment: Social Theory and the Ethics of Truth* (London: UCL Press, 1998).

18. T. H. Marshall, *Citizenship and Social Class*, ed. by T. Bottomore (1949; London: Pluto Press, 1992), pp. 3–51.

19. Nicholas B. Dirks, *Castes of Mind: Colonialism and the Making of Modern India* (Princeton: Princeton University Press, 2001).

20. K. Suresh Singh, ed., *People of India*, 43 vols. (Calcutta: Anthropological Survey of India, 1995–).

21. Partha Chatterjee, "Two Poets and Death: On Civil and Political Society in the Non-Christian World," in Tim Mitchell and Lila Abu-Lughod, eds., *Questions of Modernity* (Minneapolis: University of Minnesota Press, 2000); "Beyond the Nation? Or Within?" *Social Text*, Autumn 1998; "Community in the East," *Economic and Political Weekly*, January 1998; "The Wages of Freedom" in Partha Chatterjee, ed., *The Wages of Freedom: Fifty Years of the Indian Nation-state* (Delhi: Oxford University Press, 1998).

22. For arguments of this kind, see Jean L. Cohen and Andrew Arato, *Civil Society and Political Theory* (Cambridge: MIT Press, 1992).

23. See in particular Ranajit Guha, "On Some Aspects of the Historiography of Colonial India," *Subaltern Studies I* (Delhi: Oxford University Press, 1982), pp. 1–8.

24. I am grateful to Ashok Dasgupta and Debashis Bhattacharya of *Ajkal* for their generous help in researching the story of Balak Brahmachari's death.

25. *Ajkal*, May 18, 1993.

26. *Ajkal*, June 21, 1993.

27. *Ajkal*, June 26, 1993.

28. *Ajkal*, June 26, 1993.

29. *The Telegraph*, July 1, 1993; *The Statesman*, July 1, 1993.

30. *Ajkal*, July 2, 1993.

31. *Ajkal*, July 13, 1993.

32. *Dainik Pratibedan*, February 5, 1994.

33. Sudipta Kaviraj has explicitly formulated this as a Tocquevillian problem in "The Culture of Representative Democracy" in Partha Chatterjee, ed., *The Wages of Freedom*, pp. 147–75.

34. The writings of the *Subaltern Studies* group of historians have explored these themes most elaborately. See in particular, Ranajit Guha, *Dominance Without Hegemony* (Cambridge: Harvard University Press, 1998).

NOTES TO CHAPTER 3

1. Asok Sen, "Life and Labour in a Squatters' Colony," Occasional Paper 138, Centre for Studies in Social Sciences, Calcutta, October 1992.

2. The actual names of settlers have been changed in this account.

3. Survey conducted by SAVERA, an NGO for social welfare that runs a non-formal school, health center and vocation training center in the rail colony. I am grateful to Saugata Roy for guiding me to this survey and to the recent situation in the settlement.

4. Asok Sen, "The Bindery Workers of Daftaripara: 1. Forms and Fragments," Occasional Paper 127, Centre for Studies in Social Sciences, Calcutta, April 1991.

5. Asok Sen, "The Bindery Workers of Daftaripara: 2. Their Own Life-stories," Occasional Paper 128, Centre for Studies in Social Sciences, Calcutta, June 1991.

6. Dwaipayan Bhattacharya, "Civic Community and its Margins: School Teachers in Rural West Bengal," *Economic and Political Weekly* 36, no. 8 (February 24, 2001): 673–83.

7. Robert D. Putnam, Robert Leonardi and Raffaella Y. Nanetti, *Making Democracy Work: Civic Traditions in Modern Italy* (Princeton: Princeton University Press, 1993).

8. I am grateful to Akeel Bilgrami for suggesting this point.

9. See, in particular, Michael M. Cernea, *The Economics of Involuntary Resettlement: Questions and Challenges* (Washington, D.C.: World Bank, 1999).

10. For the most general statement, see Amartya Sen, *Development as Freedom* (New York: Random House, 1999).

11. For a sampling of discussions in India on the question of resettlement, see Jean Drèze and Veena Das, compilers, Papers on Displacement and Resettlement, presented at workshop at the Delhi School of Economics, *Economic and Political Weekly* (June 15, 1996), pp. 1453–1540.

12. Partha Chatterjee, "Recent Strategies of Resettlement and Rehabilitation in West Bengal," paper presented at the workshop on Social Development in West Bengal, Centre for Studies in Social Sciences, Calcutta, June 2000.

13. The Rajarhat acquisition case has been recently discussed in detail by Sanjay Mitra, one of the officials handling the project, in "Planned Urbanisation through Public Participation: Case of the New Town, Kolkata," *Economic and Political Weekly* 37, no. 11 (March 16, 2002): 1048–54

14. Thomas Blom Hansen, *Wages of Violence: Naming and Identity in Postcolonial Bombay* (Princeton: Princeton University Press, 2001); Aditya Nigam, "Secularism, Modernity, Nation: Epistemology of the Dalit Critique," *Economic and Political Weekly* 35, no. 48 (November 25, 2000).

15. Yogendra Yadav, "Understanding the Second Democratic Upsurge: Trends of Bahujan Participation in Electoral Politics in the 1990s" in Francine Frankel, Zoya Hasan, Rajeev Bhargava and Balveer Arora, eds., *Transforming India: Social and Political Dynamics of Democracy* (Delhi: Oxford University Press, 2000).

16. See, for example, Nivedita Menon, ed., *Gender and Politics in India* (Delhi: Oxford University Press, 1999).

NOTES TO CHAPTER 4

1. Susobhan Chandra Sarkar, *Bengal Renaissance and Other Essays* (New Delhi: People's Publishing House, 1970).

2. Barun De, "Susobhan Chandra Sarkar," in *Essays in Honour of Professor S. C. Sarkar* (New Delhi: People's Publishing House, 1976), pp. xvii–lvi.

3. Susobhanchandra Sarkar, *Mahayuddher pare iyorop* (Calcutta: University of Calcutta, 1939).

4. Karl Marx and Frederick Engels, *The Communist Manifesto* (New York: Monthly Review Press, 1998).

5. In writing the following paragraphs, I have drawn liberally from a previous Schoff lecture delivered by Saskia Sassen, *Losing Control? Sovereignty in an Age of Globalization* (New York: Columbia University Press, 1996).

6. Saskia Sassen, *The Global City: New York, London, Tokyo* (Princeton: Princeton University Press, 1991).

7. There is an apocryphal saying, attributed to the period of the Great Revolt of 1857, about the *laddus* (sweets) of Delhi that were apparently in circulation spreading the message of revolt. If one accepted them, it meant an endorsement of the revolt, thus invoking the wrath of the British. Yet if one refused them, one risked displeasing the rebels.

8. Antonio Negri and Michael Hardt, *Empire* (Cambridge: Harvard University Press, 2000).

9. The reference is to the *Ramayana* story of the squirrel who, for his love of Lord Rama, carries a little pebble to help in the construction of the great bridge across the sea to Lanka.

10. Ranajit Guha, *Dominance Without Hegemony: History and Power in Colonial India* (Cambridge: Harvard University Press, 1998).

NOTES TO CHAPTER 6

1. Madhav Govinda Vaidya, spokesman of the Rashtriya Swayamsevak Sangh (RSS) at a press conference in New Delhi, March 27, 2002. Reported in *Anandabajar Patrika* (Calcutta), 28 March 2002.

2. "Secularism and Toleration" in Partha Chatterjee, *A Possible India: Essays in Political Criticism* (Delhi: Oxford University Press, 1997), pp. 228–262.

3. *The Telegraph* (Calcutta), January 29, 2002.

4. *Times of India* (Calcutta), January 31, 2002.

5. *Times of India*, January 30, 2002.

6. *Times of India*, February 1, 2002.

7. *Times of India*, February 2, 2002.

8. *Times of India*, February 3, 2002.

9. *Times of India*, February 5, 2002.

10. *Ganashakti* (Calcutta), February 5, 2002.

11. *Times of India*, February 7, 2002.

12. *Ganashakti*, February 7, 2002.

13. *The Telegraph*, February 8, 2002; *Anandabajar Patrika*, February 8, 2002; *Ganashakti*, February 8, 2002; *Times of India*, February 8, 2002.

14. *Times of India*, February 12, 2002.

15. Milan Datta, "Madrasar biruddhe prachar: Age satyata jene nin," *Anandabajar Patrika*, January 29, 2002; *The Telegraph*, January 30, 2002.

16. *Anandabajar Patrika*, January 29, 2002.

17. Anisur Rahaman, "Ladener roja," *Ganashakti*, January 29, 2002.

18. *Times of India*, February 1, 2002.

19. *The Telegraph*, February 1, 2002.

20. *Anandabajar Patrika*, February 1, 2002.

21. Mainul Hasan, "Madrasah shiksha: bartaman samay o Muslim samaj," *Ganashakti*, 6 February 2002.

22. *The Telegraph*, February 12, 2002.

23. Letter by Fatema Begum, Bagnan, Howrah, in *Anandabajar Patrika*, February 28, 2002.

NOTES TO CHAPTER 7

1. Dipesh Chakrabarty, *Rethinking Working-Class History: Bengal 1890–1940* (Delhi: Oxford University Press, 1989).

2. For a statistical analysis based on the 1961 Census, see Arabinda Biswas, Partha Chatterjee and Shibanikinkar Chaube, "The Ethnic Composition of Calcutta and the Residential Pattern of Minorities," *Geographical Review of India* 38, 2 (June 1976): 140–66.

3. Nirmal Kumar Bose, *Calcutta 1964: A Social Survey* (Bombay: Lalvani, 1968).

4. Nirmal Kumar Bose, "Calcutta: A Premature Metropolis," *Scientific American* 213, no 3: 91–102.

5. Chakrabarty, *Rethinking Working-Class History*.

6. Thomas Blom Hansen, *Wages of Violence: Naming and Identity in Postcolonial Bombay* (Princeton: Princeton University Press, 2001).

7. Gyan Prakash, "The Urban Turn" in *Sarai Reader 02: The Cities of Everyday Life* (Delhi: Sarai, 2002), pp. 2–7.

8. Ma [Mahendranath Gupta], *Srisriramkrishna kathamrita* (1902–32; reprint, Calcutta: Ananda, 1983).

9. Bhabanicharan Bandyopadhyay, *Kalikata kamalalay* (1823; reprint, Calcutta: Nabapatra, 1987).

10. See, for instance, the discussion in Pradip Kumar Bose, "Sons of the Nation" in Partha Chatterjee, ed., *Texts of Power: Emerging Disciplines in Colonial Bengal* (Minneapolis: University of Minnesota Press, 1995), pp. 118–144.

11. There is now a large literature on the new global cities. See, for example, Saskia Sassen, *The Global City: New York, London, Tokyo* (Princeton: Princeton University Press, 1991).

12. All the above figures are from a CMDA survey carried out in 1996: Nandita Chatterjee, Nikhilesh Bhattacharya and Animesh Halder, *Socioeconomic Profile of Households in Calcutta Metropolitan Area* (Calcutta: Calcutta Metropolitan Development Authority, 1999).

Bibliography

EUROPEAN LANGUAGE SOURCES

Newspapers

Columbia University Record (New York).
The Statesman (Calcutta).
The Telegraph (Calcutta).
The Times of India (Calcutta).

Books and Articles

Abu-Lughod, Ibrahim. *Arab Rediscovery of Europe: A Study in Cultural Encounters.* Princeton: Princeton University Press, 1963.

Ambedkar, B. R. *Pakistan or the Partition of India.* 2nd ed. Bombay: Thacker, 1945.

———. *Who Were the Shudras? How They Came to be the Fourth Varna in the Indo-Aryan Society.* 1946; reprint, Bombay: Thackers, 1970.

———. *The Untouchables: Who Were They and Why They Became Untouchables.* New Delhi: Amrit Book Company, 1948.

Amin, Shahid. "Gandhi as Mahatma" in Ranajit Guha, ed. *Subaltern Studies III.* Delhi: Oxford University Press, 1984, pp. 1–61.

———. *Event, Metaphor, Memory: Chauri Chaura 1922–1992.* Delhi: Oxford University Press, 1995.

Anderson, Benedict. *Imagined Communities: Reflections on the Origin and Spread of Nationalism.* London: Verso, 1983.

———. *The Spectre of Comparisons: Nationalism, Southeast Asia and the World.* London: Verso, 1998.

Avineri, Shlomo and Avner de-Shalit, eds. *Communitarianism and Individualism*. Oxford: Oxford University Press, 1992.

Balibar, Étienne. *Masses, Classes, Ideas: Studies on Politics and Philosophy Before and After Marx*. New York: Routledge, 1994.

Bhabha, Homi. "DissemiNation" in Bhabha, ed. *Nation and Narration*. London: Routledge, 1990, pp. 291–322.

Bhattacharya, Dwaipayan. "Civic Community and its Margins: School Teachers in Rural West Bengal." *Economic and Political Weekly* 36, 8. (February 24, 2001): 673–83.

Biswas, Arabinda, Partha Chatterjee and Shibanikinkar Chaube. "The Ethnic Composition of Calcutta and the Residential Pattern of Minorities." *Geographical Review of India*, 38, 2 (June 1976): 140–166.

Bose, Nirmal Kumar. *Calcutta 1964: A Social Survey*. Bombay: Lalvani, 1968.

———. "Calcutta: A Premature Metropolis." *Scientific American* 213, no. 3: 91–102.

Bose, Pradip Kumar. "Sons of the Nation." In Partha Chatterjee, ed. *Texts of Power: Emerging Disciplines in Colonial Bengal*. Minneapolis: University of Minnesota Press, 1995, pp. 118–44.

Cernea, Michael M. *The Economics of Involuntary Resettlement: Questions and Challenges*. Washington, D.C.: World Bank, 1999.

Chakrabarty, Dipesh. *Rethinking Working-Class History: Bengal 1890–1940*. Delhi: Oxford University Press, 1989.

Chatterjee, Nandita, Nikhilesh Bhattacharya and Animesh Halder, *Socioeconomic Profile of Households in Calcutta Metropolitan Area*. Calcutta: Calcutta Metropolitan Development Authority, 1999.

Chatterjee, Partha. "Two Poets and Death: On Civil and Political Society in the Non-Christian World." In Tim Mitchell, eds. *Questions of Modernity*. Minneapolis: University of Minnesota Press, 2000, pp. 35–48.

———. "Beyond the Nation? Or Within?" *Social Text* 56 (Fall 1998): 57–69.

———. "Community in the East." *Economic and Political Weekly* 33, 6 (February 7, 1998): 277–82.

———. "The Wages of Freedom." In Partha Chatterjee, ed. *Wages of Freedom: Fifty Years of the Indian Nation-state*. Delhi: Oxford University Press, 1998, pp. 1–20.

———. *A Possible India: Essays in Political Criticism*. Delhi: Oxford University Press, 1997.

———. "Recent Strategies of Resettlement and Rehabilitation in West Bengal." paper presented at the workshop on Social Development in

West Bengal, Centre for Studies in Social Sciences, Calcutta, June 2000.

Cohen, Jean L. and Andrew Arato. *Civil Society and Political Theory.* Cambridge: MIT Press, 1992.

Collet, Sophia Dobson. *The Life and Letters of Raja Rammohun Roy,* ed. Dilip Kumar Biswas and Prabhat Chandra Ganguli. 1900; reprint, Calcutta: Sadharan Brahmo Samaj, 1962.

De, Barun. "Susobhan Chandra Sarkar." In *Essays in Honour of Professor S. C. Sarkar.* New Delhi: People's Publishing House, 1976, pp. xvii–lvi.

Dirks, Nicholas B. *Castes of Mind: Colonialism and the Making of Modern India.* Princeton: Princeton University Press, 2001.

Drèze, Jean and Veena Das, compilers, Papers on Displacement and Resettlement, presented at workshop at the Delhi School of Economics, *Economic and Political Weekly* (June 15, 1996): 1453–1540.

Foucault, Michel. "Different Spaces." In James D. Faubion, ed. *Essential Works of Foucault,* vol. 2: *Aesthetics, Method and Epistemology.* New York: New Press, 1998, pp. 175–85.

———. "Governmentality." In Graham Burchell, Colin Gordon and Peter Miller, eds. *The Foucault Effect: Studies in Governmentality.* Chicago: University of Chicago Press, 1991, pp. 87–104.

Galanter, Marc. *Competing Equalities: Law and the Backward Classes in India.* Delhi: Oxford University Press, 1984.

Guha, Ranajit. "On Some Aspects of the Historiography of Colonial India." *Subaltern Studies I.* Delhi: Oxford University Press, 1982, pp. 1–8.

———. *Dominance Without Hegemony: History and Power in Colonial India.* Cambridge: Harvard University Press, 1998.

Hacking, Ian. *The Taming of Chance.* Cambridge: Cambridge University Press, 1990.

Hansen, Thomas Blom. *Wages of Violence: Naming and Identity in Postcolonial Bombay.* Princeton: Princeton University Press, 2001.

Hardiman, David. *The Coming of the Devi: Adivasi Assertion in Western India.* Delhi: Oxford University Press, 1987.

James, C. L. R. *The Black Jacobins: Toussaint L'Ouverture and the San Domingo Revolution.* New York: Vintage Books, 1963.

Kausar, Kabir. *Secret Correspondence of Tipu Sultan.* New Delhi: Light and Life, 1980.

Kaviraj, Sudipta. "The Culture of Representative Democracy." In Partha Chatterjee, ed. *Wages of Freedom: Fifty Years of the Indian Nation-State.* Delhi: Oxford University Press, 1998, pp. 147–75.

Kumar, Ravinder. "Gandhi, Ambedkar and the Poona Pact, 1932." In Jim Masselos, ed. *Struggling and Ruling: The Indian National Congress, 1885–1985.* New Delhi: Sterling, 1987.

Marshall, T. H. *Citizenship and Social Class,* ed. by T. Bottomore ([1949]; London: Pluto Press, 1992, pp. 3–51.

Marx, Karl "On the Jewish Question" [1843]. In Karl Marx and Frederick Engels, *Collected Works,* vol. 3. Moscow: Progress Publishers, 1975, pp. 146–74.

———. *Capital,* vol. 1, tr. Samuel Moore and Edward Aveling [1868] Moscow: Progress Publishers, 1954, pp. 667–724.

———. "The British Rule in India." [1853] In Karl Marx and Frederick Engels, *Collected Works,* vol. 12. Moscow: Progress Publishers, 1979, pp. 125–33.

———. *The Ethnological Notebooks,* ed. by Lawrence Krader. Assen: Van Gorcum, 1974.

——— and Frederick Engels, *The Communist Manifesto.* New York: Monthly Review Press, 1998.

Menon, Nivedita, ed. *Gender and Politics in India.* Delhi: Oxford University Press, 1999.

Miller, Peter and Nikolas Rose, "Production, Identity and Democracy." *Theory and Society,* 24 (1995): 427–67.

Mitchell, Timothy. *Colonising Egypt.* Cambridge: Cambridge University Press, 1988.

Mitra, Sanjay. "Planned Urbanisation through Public Participation: Case of the New Town, Kolkata." *Economic and Political Weekly* 37, no. 11 (March 16, 2002): 1048–54.

Negri. Antonio and Michael Hardt, *Empire.* Cambridge: Harvard University Press, 2000.

Nigam, Aditya. "Secularism, Modernity, Nation: Epistemology of the Dalit Critique." *Economic and Political Weekly* 35, no. 48 (November 25, 2000.

Omvedt, Gail. *Dalits and the Democratic Revolution: Dr. Ambedkar and the Dalit Movement in Colonial India.* New Delhi: Sage, 1994.

Osborne, Thomas. *Aspects of Enlightenment: Social Theory and the Ethics of Truth.* London: UCL Press, 1998.

Pettit, Philip. *Republicanism: A Theory of Freedom and Government.* Oxford: Oxford University Press, 1997.

Poovey, Mary. *Making a Social Body.* Chicago: University of Chicago Press, 1995.

———. *A History of the Modern Fact.* Chicago: University of Chicago Press, 1998.

Prakash, Gyan. "The Urban Turn." In *Sarai Reader 02: The Cities of Everyday Life.* Delhi: Sarai, 2002, pp. 2–7.

Putnam, Robert D., Robert Leonardi and Raffaella Y. Nanetti, *Making Democracy Work: Civic Traditions in Modern Italy.* Princeton: Princeton University Press, 1993.

Rose, Nikolas. *Powers of Freedom: Reframing Political Thought.* Cambridge: Cambridge University Press, 1999.

Sandel, Michael, ed. *Liberalism and Its Critics.* New York: New York University Press, 1984.

Sarkar, Susobhan Chandra. *Bengal Renaissance and Other Essays.* New Delhi: People's Publishing House, 1970.

Sassen, Saskia. *Losing Control? Sovereignty in an Age of Globalization.* New York: Columbia University Press, 1996.

———. *The Global City: New York, London, Tokyo.* Princeton: Princeton University Press, 1991.

Sen, Amartya. *Development as Freedom.* New York: Random House, 1999.

Sen, Asok. "The Bindery Workers of Daftaripara: 1. Forms and Fragments." Occasional Paper 127, Centre for Studies in Social Sciences, Calcutta, April 1991.

———. "The Bindery Workers of Daftaripara: 2. Their Own Life-stories." Occasional Paper 128, Centre for Studies in Social Sciences, Calcutta, June 1991.

———. "Life and Labour in a Squatters' Colony." Occasional Paper 138, Centre for Studies in Social Sciences, Calcutta, October 1992.

Shanin, Teodor. *Late Marx and the Russian Road: Marx and 'the Peripheries of Capitalism'.* London: Routledge and Kegan Paul, 1983.

Shourie, Arun. *Worshipping False Gods: Ambedkar and the Facts Which Have Been Erased.* New Delhi: ASA Publications, 1997.

Singh, K. Suresh, ed. *People of India,* 43 vols.. Calcutta: Anthropological Survey of India, 1995- .

Skinner, Quentin. *Liberty Before Liberalism.* Cambridge: Cambridge University Press, 1997.

Srinivas, M. N. *Social Change in Modern India.* Berkeley: University of California Press, 1966.

Trouillot, Michel-Rolph. *Silencing the Past: Power and the Production of History.* Boston: Beacon Press, 1995.

Viswanathan, Gauri. *Outside the Fold: Conversion, Modernity, and Belief.* Princeton: Princeton University Press, 1998.

Yadav, Yogendra. "Understanding the Second Democratic Upsurge: Trends of Bahujan Participation in Electoral Politics in the 1990s." In Francine Frankel, Zoya Hasan, Rajeev Bhargava, and Balveer Arora, eds. *Transforming India: Social and Political Dynamics of Democracy.* Delhi: Oxford University Press, 2000.

BENGALI LANGUAGE SOURCES

Newspapers

Ajkal (Calcutta).
Anandabajar Patrika (Calcutta).
Dainik Pratibedan (Calcutta).
Ganashakti (Calcutta).

Books and Articles

Bandyopadhyay, Bhabanicharan. *Kalikata kamalalay.* 1823; reprint, Calcutta: Nabapatra, 1987.

Bhaduri, Satinath. *Dhorai charitmanas* (vol. 1, 1949; vol. 2, 1951) in Sankha Ghosh and Nirmalya Acharya, eds. *Satinath granthabali*, vol. 2. Calcutta: Signet, 1973, pp. 1–296.

Datta, Milan. "Madrasar biruddhe prachar: Age satyata jene nin." *Anandabajar Patrika*, 29 January 2002.

Hasan, Mainul. "Madrasah shiksha: bartaman samay o Muslim samaj." *Ganashakti*, 6 February 2002.

Ma [Mahendranath Gupta], *Srisriramkrishna kathamrita* (1902–32; reprint, Calcutta: Ananda, 1983.

Rahaman,, Anisur. "Ladener roja." *Ganashakti*, 29 January 2002.

Sarkar, Susobhanchandra. *Mahayuddher pare iyorop.* Calcutta: University of Calcutta, 1939.

Index

Srinivas, M. N., 12
Subaltern Studies, 39–40
Sukhchar, 43–4
Syria, 109, 150

Taliban, 110
Tatma, 10, 11, 12
Telegraph, The, 45
terrorism, 108, 114–17, 120, 129–30,
   150
Thackeray, Bal, 117
Tipu Sultan, 27–28
Tocqueville, Alexis de, 48
Tokyo, 90
tribes, 37: scheduled, 57
Trinamul Congress, 60
Trouillot, Michel-Rolph, 29
Tulsidas, 10
Turkey, 21, 96

United Nations, 98, 149–52
United States of America, 35, 85,
   88, 96, 98, 107: its empire, 96,
   97–100, 109, 123, 150; at war,

108–11, 114–15, 116, 118, 129,
   149–52
Urdu, 117, 133

Vajpayee, A.B., 115
Vietnam, 82

Wales, 94
Washington, 104
Weber, Max, 33
West: modern, 3, 27
West Bengal, 41, 61, 71, 115, 127–
   29, 145–46: madrasahs in, 116–
   27; panchayats in, 44, 65–7; *see
   also* Bengal; Calcutta
West Indies, 87
Wolfowitz, Paul, 150
World Bank, 68, 134
World Trade Center, 111: *see also*
   September 11 events
World War I, 81, 85, 87
World War II, 81, 85, 87, 93, 108

Yugoslavia, 99